POSITIVE DISCIPLINE FOR KIDS

THE ESSENTIAL GUIDE TO MANAGE CHILDREN'S BEHAVIOUR, DEVELOP EFFECTIVE COMMUNICATION AND RAISE A POSITIVE AND CONFIDENT CHILD

JOANNA WELLS

© **Copyright Wryting Ltd 2020 - All rights reserved.**

The content contained within this book may not be reproduced, duplicated or transmitted without direct written permission from the author or the publisher.

Under no circumstances will any blame or legal responsibility be held against the publisher, or author, for any damages, reparation, or monetary loss due to the information contained within this book, either directly or indirectly.

Legal Notice:

This book is copyright protected. It is only for personal use. You cannot amend, distribute, sell, use, quote or paraphrase any part, or the content within this book, without the consent of the author or publisher.

Disclaimer Notice:

Please note the information contained within this document is for educational and entertainment purposes only. All effort has been executed to present accurate, up to date, reliable, complete information. No warranties of any kind are declared or implied. Readers acknowledge that the author is not engaged in the rendering of legal, financial, medical or professional advice. The content within this book has been derived from various sources. Please consult a licensed professional before attempting any techniques outlined in this book.

By reading this document, the reader agrees that under no circumstances is the author responsible for any losses, direct or indirect, that are incurred as a result of the use of the information contained within this document, including, but not limited to, errors, omissions, or inaccuracies.

CONTENTS

Introduction   5

1. Sometimes It's Not Them, It's You   13
2. Digging Deeper into Discipline   31
3. The Core of Positive Discipline   41
4. A Different Approach   60
5. Guiding Your Child's Behavior   77
6. Developing Effective Communication   88
7. Raising Positive, Confident Kids   97

Conclusion   111
References   123

This Positive Discipline checklist includes:

- 10 essential concepts you need to be aware of to help you maintain the best environment for your child.
- Including three high-quality product recommendations that you can use to help you get the most from your child's behaviour.
- Where you can buy these items for the lowest price.

To receive your essential Positive Discipline checklist, visit the link:

http://joannawells.com/checklist/

INTRODUCTION

Our children are our future. But what kind of future would that be if we sent them into it unprepared and without a sense of structure and discipline?

As a parent or caregiver, your most important job is to teach your child to behave in a manner that is acceptable to society. It takes time and patience, and learning healthy and effective discipline strategies will go a long way toward helping you raise an emotionally healthy, positive, and confident child.

What Is Discipline?

When you think of the word, "discipline", what comes to mind? Do you think about punishment, or do you think about teaching?

The majority of people would say that it's a bit of both. They would agree that discipline is a way to teach a child to follow the rules and adhere to specific standards of behaviour. It is when it comes to the method of enforcing or teaching discipline that people do not always have similar views. The most common belief about discipline is that it should be enforced by using punishment. Some also believe that good behaviour is rewarded in some way or another.

When we teach our children the difference between acceptable and unacceptable behaviour by rewarding them when they behave well and punishing them when they do not, we trust that we are doing what is best for our child, but is that really true? What does a child learn when they are bribed with a reward to behave in a certain way? And what do they learn from being punished?

To answer these questions, let's take a look at the meaning of punishment as it relates to child discipline. Punishment can mean anything from time-out, taking away privileges, and physical punishment to yelling, scolding, withholding affection, or humiliating the child. As you can see, all of these punishments are intentionally unpleasant in some way or other. The psychology behind this is that the child will stop the inappropriate behaviour and start displaying the desired behaviour to avoid the unpleasant experience of punishment. Doesn't that sound a bit like conditioning to you rather than teaching?

It becomes clear that the "punishment and reward" system does not teach the child any substantial values. It is what is called "enforcing discipline," with the emphasis on the word, *"enforce"*. The idea is that the child will change their behaviour to the desired behaviour out of fear of retribution or even physical pain or discomfort.

This method satisfies the parent or authority figure. They are happy because they have achieved a certain desired end-result. But is that really what you want your child to be? An end result? I very much doubt that. We all want our children to grow up to be healthy, balanced, and happy adults.

You may even look back at your childhood at some point and remember how you were disciplined. You may even proudly say things like, "When I was a kid, I had to do as I was told or I would get the belt, and I'm fine today." You may be right. You may be fine today, but when you think about it, are you really?

Do you think that you may have benefited from a different kind of discipline where you learned through kindness and encouragement?

What Makes Positive Discipline Different?

Contrary to what you may believe, positive discipline is not a positive means of punishing children for misbehaving. Positive discipline does not mean handing out praise and presents for good behaviour and taking away toys or giving time-out for bad behaviour. Research has proven that these methods are not effective in the long term and could even harm family relationships and the child's emotional development.

All children have a fundamental need to feel significant and to belong, but they often have a mistaken belief of how to go about gaining that sense of belonging and feeling of importance. When a child is feeling neglected and rejected, they tend to misbehave to gain attention and acceptance. It is easy to misinterpret this and simply see it as the child being naughty, disobedient, or just plain difficult, so we react by reprimanding and punishing the child, unknowingly confirming their feeling that they are unacceptable or do not belong.

On the other side of the coin, when a child has been good, we tend to make a fuss and reward the child as though they have achieved something extraordinary. This could cause them to believe that good or correct behaviour is extraordinary rather than expected and that it must be rewarded when it is achieved.

We need to keep in mind that each person has their own perception of the world, and children even more so. They are not yet jaded and faded by the harsh realities of life, so they tend to look at it from a surprisingly different perception than what we do. Let's take a look at a few examples of how their beliefs are created.

It's bedtime, and you've reminded your five-year-old several times now to pack up their toys and get ready for bed. They acknowledge you, but they carry on playing, making no move to do as you asked.

You've had a long day, and you're not in the mood for this. You lose your cool and start picking up the toys, throwing them into the toy box, sparing each toy little mercy. Your little one is startled and frightened by your sudden violent action. Their lower lip begins to quiver while huge tears start rolling down their cheeks. Your irritation makes you less than reasonable, and when you see the tears, you do a mental facepalm and think, "Oh no, not the waterworks again." You yell at them to stop bawling, leave the toys, and just go to bed. You add things like, "Why don't you listen? Why is it so hard to get you to do as I say? You drive me crazy!"

The child does what you wanted, but you are left with the last few toys on the floor and an empty feeling in your heart. They are upset and crying, and you're feeling like a monster. You go to them and apologize. You explain that you've had a hard day. You're tired and you've got a headache.

A belief has begun to form in your five-year-old's mind that yelling and throwing things about is okay when you're tired and irritated. They also learn that you get what you want when you throw a tantrum.

Or, let's do it another way. We have precisely the same scenario as above; only you don't lose your cool - you don't even have the energy for that. After the third or fourth time of being ignored, you just let it go and decide to try again in half an hour. Maybe they are in the mood to listen then. This scenario is way more peaceful, but nothing has been achieved. Or is it really nothing? And if something has been achieved, is it good? Let's take a look.

By giving up and not pursuing the matter you have managed to instil a belief in your child that you will stop nagging if they ignore you for long enough. Once again, not quite the intended lesson, is it?

Let's look at another possibility—the reward. We have the same scene as before, only you don't lose your cool, and you don't let them be and wait for half an hour. You bribe them. You tell them that they can have one of their favourite cookies if they are "good" and pick up their toys. They decide that the cookie sounds better than toys right now, so they comply. You give them the cookie, tell them how good they are, and everybody is happy for now. You got what you wanted but you have lost your power. Now they believe that they must be rewarded for doing as you ask and will most likely insist on another cookie when you tell them it's bedtime.

You may think that discipline is about getting your child to follow the rules and to display appropriate behaviour by any means that seems to work for you, but discipline is not just about the end result. Each time you discipline a child, whether you do it in a positive, negative, or passive manner, a belief is created in their mind relevant to your actions. Have you instilled a sense of fear instead of respect? Have you created feelings of resentment and rebellion instead of acceptance and cooperation? Have you taught them that they are entitled to rewards for good behaviour? Remember, there's a huge difference between positive attention when your child behaves and rewarding them for good behaviour.

These are very simple examples, but it is clear to see that none of them gives us the desired result. The child has not learnt anything positive. Instead, mistaken beliefs have been created in their mind, and their future behaviour will reflect these.

Now let's try one more scenario. You've asked your five-year-old to pick up their toys and get ready for bed and while they acknowledge you, they keep on playing. You go to them and say: "I can see that you're enjoying your toys, but it's time to pack them up now and get ready for bed. Remember, we agreed that six o'clock is pyjama-time? Let's say good night to your toys and put them in the toy box together, and then we'll get you into your jammies." You make a game of saying good night to the toys as you start packing them up and they join in. There was no conflict, no bribery, and no confusion. You have kindly and gently reminded your child that you agreed about pyjama-time and you helped them make the right choice through your actions.

Positive discipline is based on the principle that there are no bad kids, just good and bad behaviour. It focuses on the positive points of the child's behaviour and teaches them to make better choices. Positive discipline is a respectful, encouraging way to teach children the essential social and life skills they need to become valuable and resourceful members of their communities.

1

SOMETIMES IT'S NOT THEM, IT'S YOU

We would do well to remember that children are always listening and learning, whether consciously or subconsciously. A child is like a sponge that absorbs everything around it, and as it is absorbed, the information is processed and turned into thoughts and beliefs. Your child learned to speak by repeating your words, and in the same way, they learn how to behave by repeating your behaviour.

If you are a happy-go-lucky free spirit, chances are your child will have many of those same traits. If you are polite and show others compassion, your child is very likely to do the same. But unfortunately, it works both ways. If you are short-tempered, lose your cool easily, yell often, or even strike your child, do not be surprised if this is how they behave and treat their siblings, peers, and even you. They are merely emulating your behaviour.

Discipline is not the one-way process we sometimes imagine it to be. Discipline is an interaction between two people with the parent as the teacher and the child as the learner. It's a two-way process, and this is why we need to take a look at you, the parent. Let's find out who you are and how your behaviour and management of your child's misbehaviour can influence them. Are you ready?

PARENTING STYLES

Just like our kids, parents are unique individuals, each with their frame of reference, different backgrounds, different upbringings, and different perceptions of discipline, so it makes sense that no two parents will raise their children in the same way.

However, there are enough common factors and similarities in the way parents raise and discipline their kids to allow psychologists to group them into what they refer to as "parenting styles." The original studies that were done in the 1960s identified three parenting styles. These were authoritarian, authoritative, and permissive. Further studies proved that there was a fourth style, and uninvolved parenting was added.

It is important to remember that a parenting style is not a specific characteristic or personality trait of a parent. Your parenting style does not define who you are as a parent or person; it defines how you are disciplining your child. A parenting style describes the combination of strategies and techniques that parents use to raise their children - to put it very simply, a parenting style is a pattern of behaviour displayed when a parent is disciplining a child.

Your child's behaviour can also influence your parenting style. Studies have shown that children who persistently display difficult or aggressive behaviour can cause parents to eventually give up and allow the child to do as they please. Sometimes it's merely a matter of what you're doing is not working for that particular child. Each parent and each child is different, making it an impossible task to pin down an exact strategy that will work every time for everyone.

It must also be kept in mind that there is usually more than one person involved in the discipline of a child, and differing parenting styles can cause confusion. Whether the parents live together or not, they must cooperate and agree on how they plan to combine their parenting styles to the greatest benefit of their child.

Authoritarian Parenting

You believe that children should be seen and not heard. Your rules are your rules—you don't have to explain them. Discipline is enforced through punishment. Children don't have opinions—they do as you say.

Authoritarian parenting is all about strict rules and control. Failure to follow the rules and making mistakes are treated harshly and almost always results in some or other form of punishment. Many authoritarian parents also believe that corporal punishment is a necessary form of enforcing discipline and will not hesitate to smack or spank their children to "get them back in line" when they misbehave. These parents expect their kids to obey their orders without questioning and this provides the child with very little direction on how to avoid making the same mistake in the future. Sometimes the child is left confused and wondering what exactly it is that they did wrong.

As teenagers, these kids are likely to be obedient and competent but will lack some of the communication and social skills that are required for leadership. They will probably have low self-esteem and not be truly happy. As adults, they tend to become authoritarian like their parents, both in their personal relationships and when they become parents themselves.

Authoritative Parenting

When you make rules, you explain the reasons behind the rules. You consider your child's opinion when enforcing rules and giving consequences. You validate your child's feelings, but it is still clear who is in charge.

Authoritative parents set limits and boundaries while at the same time encouraging their kids to be independent. They are usually reasonable, fair, and just, and because of this, their children are more likely to obey them.

When these kids make mistakes and fail to meet expectations, their parents are supportive and nurturing. They will forgive rather than punish. These parents are assertive but not restrictive or intrusive. They are responsive to their children and listen to their questions.

Authoritative parents tend to give their children more independence as they grow older and this creates a higher leadership potential. These kids have better social skills, self-control and self-reliance, and make good employees, employers, and life partners.

Permissive Parenting

You have some vague rules that are seldom enforced, and consequences are rare. However, you will step in when there is a serious problem. Your child sees you as a friend.

Permissive parenting is sometimes also referred to as indulgent parenting. These parents usually have an "anything goes" attitude. They are warm and interactive and behave more like friends than parents. They rarely discipline their children and there are very few rules and boundaries. When they do use consequences, they often don't follow through and will reduce time-out periods or withdraw a punishment such as giving back electronics if the child appears to be sorry or even nags persistently enough.

A lack of boundaries and structure can make a child feel insecure and cause them to act out. These kids usually display a strong sense of entitlement and lack of self-control. They are likely to have problems with authority and perform poorly in school.

Uninvolved Parenting

Your child's school and homework is their business. Children should amuse themselves. You are not there to entertain them. You don't care about rules as long as they don't drag you into it if they get into trouble.

Uninvolved parenting is the fourth parenting style. It is also called neglectful parenting. These parents have few demands and are unresponsive. There is very little communication between them and their kids. They fulfil their children's basic physical needs but offer nothing in the way of guidance, support, or structure. These children end up with a lack of self-control, have low self-esteem and are socially inept because they have no idea what behaviour is appropriate and what is not.

Now that you have a general idea of what discipline is about, and what influences its effectiveness, let's take a look at how we sometimes stand in our way when it comes to effectively disciplining our children.

ARE YOU STANDING IN YOUR OWN WAY?

It is not possible to make a comprehensive list of all the things parents consciously and subconsciously say and do that defeat the purpose they hope to achieve when they discipline their kids.

We have agreed that the purpose of discipline is not getting our kids to obey us, but to teach them responsibility, appropriate behaviour and self-control, among other things. Sometimes, in our effort to make our child obey us, we forget where the focus should be. It becomes about what we want and not about what the child needs to learn. We become frustrated because nothing seems to work in the long term and our child remains confused about what it is that we really want from them.

Let's take a look at some of the things we do:

Confusing discipline with punishment: Discipline teaches the difference between right and wrong. It helps to develop self-esteem and self-control. Punishment does not teach alternative behaviour—it merely programs a person to behave in a certain way. Once the threat of retribution is out of the way, the behaviour could return to its original state. Punishment can also harm the relationship between the parent and child and cause anger and resentment in the child.

Believing if it works once, then it should work all the time: Children grow and develop, and you need to keep up with them when it comes to discipline, in the same way, you have to keep buying them bigger clothes! As they get older, you need different discipline strategies, and children with different personalities also may respond in different ways.

Thinking you are a bad parent because you're struggling with disciplining your child: This is a common trap for parents to fall into. Children are not the easiest little creatures in the world, and they change as fast as they grow. When you don't get the results you want, take a step back, think it through, and try a different approach.

Believing that you must win every battle: Sometimes you just have a feeling that you're going into a battle that you're not going to win. If it's not going to make a crucial difference to the child's development and emotional wellbeing, it may not be worth fighting about. At times, it's better to back off and let things be. The moral here is "save your battles for things that matter."

Disagreeing about discipline in the presence of a child: Settle disagreements about discipline when the child is not present and don't interfere while a child is being disciplined even if you don't agree. When adults interfere and argue about how a child should be disciplined in their presence, it confuses them and will do more damage than the "wrong discipline." It is better to discuss it when the child is not present and decide together what should be done in future.

Making empty threats: Imagine you and your partner are over at a friend's place for dinner, and you've brought the kids along. Everything is going well, but then, just before your hostess starts dishing up, your kids start arguing and fighting with each other. You tell them to stop but they just carry on. Out of desperation, you yell at them: "If you don't stop this, we're going home." Your partner rolls their eyes at you. Both of you know that going home at this stage is out of the question. The kids know it too, so they stop for a few seconds because your yelling startled them, but then they carry on. Your hostess manages to distract them by offering them a pre-dinner snack. The number of mixed messages sent in this scenario is hard to count. The kids were not only threatened with something that they knew wasn't going to happen, they were bribed into behaving! Empty threats take away your power.

KEEPING YOUR COOL WHEN YOU'RE READY TO EXPLODE

Parenting can be frustrating at times, and kids seem to have a knack for learning very quickly, which of our buttons to push. Whether it's about being ready on time, eating their dinner, "forgetting" to do chores, or talking back at some point, they're going to manage to push you to a point where you lose your cool. We all have limits and it's okay to lose your cool occasionally, but it should not be something that happens regularly.

To be clear, "losing your cool" refers to getting angry to the point of yelling at your child, maybe slamming things on the kitchen counter, or some other display of temper. If your anger pushes you to a point where you find that you become aggressive towards your child and could possibly harm them physically, please seek professional help. There is no shame in admitting that you have a problem, but there is a lot of shame in hiding it and hurting your child.

Losing your temper may be scary to a younger child and may get them going or make them stop talking back for the moment, but it has no long-term effect. They will do it again when they have forgotten your anger because they have learnt nothing. An older child might take you on verbally, and often the original problem gets forgotten in the heat of the argument and remains unsolved.

What Makes You Lose It?

Before we can look at how we can control our anger so that we don't negatively impact our kids, let's take a look at what causes us to become angry. No, this is not going to be a list of things kids do. Kids are just kids and their intent is seldom to incur our wrath. But their behaviour can trigger specific reactions in us, and some behaviours can make us lose our cool before we realize what is happening.

Once we learn to be aware of the factors that influence our own behaviour, we can learn to take them into consideration in a difficult situation with our child.

Let's take a look at the possibilities. You've got financial pressure. You've got work pressure. You've got a boss that nitpicks all day. You've got appointments, meetings, deadlines, rude customers, and inefficient service delivery to deal with. The list goes on. We tend to carry these things with us wherever we go, and the daily stresses of survival become part of our life at home and eventually impacts how we treat our family members and discipline our children.

It's not really the fact that little Janet can't find her sneaker and you're already late that triggers your temper. If you think about it, you're already frustrated with all the other things. Now your child comes with this problem and manages to add the straw that breaks the proverbial camel's back, and you fly off the handle in a fit of rage that goes way beyond what the situation warrants. If you had your own frustrations in check, your child's missing sneaker would have been a minor issue. Kids misplace things all the time and you were already running late, so another minute or two to sort out the shoe problem wouldn't have made that much of a difference. If you'd been calm and in control, you probably would have simply sighed, maybe rolled your eyes slightly, and helped her find it or suggested that she wear something else.

It's not just the stresses of day-to-day life that can push us past the point of reason and make us yell and throw tantrums at our kids. Our own childhood experiences have a lot to do with how we react to our children's behaviour. In the heat of the moment, parents might fall into the same communication patterns that they learnt when they were growing up, so they will give kids the silent treatment, yell at them, swear, call them names, be sarcastic, and more.

How does it affect your child when you lose your temper with them?

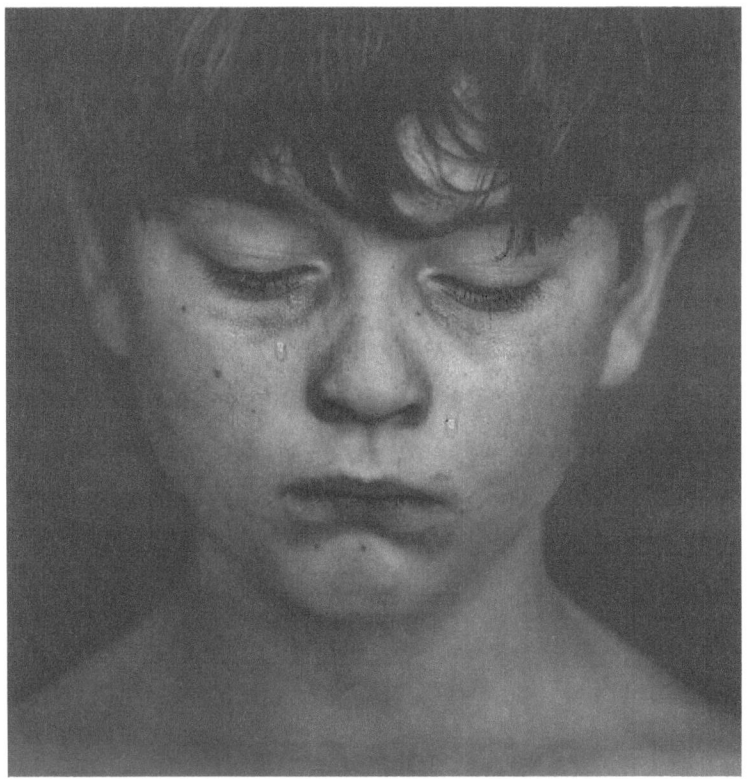

Have you ever thought about what it feels like to a little child when you yell at them? Maybe you were yelled at as a child. Maybe one of your parents smacked you on occasion. Can you remember what it felt like? Usually, you can't summon those feelings, because deep down inside, you don't want to remember them, but we're going to try to give you an idea.

Imagine you were entirely dependent on your spouse or partner for your food, safety, protection and shelter. To you, that person is the centre of your universe, your everything. They are your primary source of love. Their opinion of you creates your self-image.

Now, imagine that you've done something they don't like, and it has made them angry. Now make-believe that they are three times your size. The person that is your source of love and protection is towering over you, and they are looking threatening and scary. Their face is flushed, and they're yelling at you, spitting with each word. You don't hear everything because there's a whooshing sound in your ears, but the words that do come through are "stupid, irresponsible, irritating", and "a bloody nuisance." You aren't sure whether they are going to calm down or get angry enough to strike you. How does that make you feel? Close your eyes, imagine the scene and make an effort to summon up a genuine feeling.

Now take that feeling and magnify it by about a thousand times, and you will have an inkling of what it feels like to a child when you lose your temper and take it out on them.

Some parents will blame the child for the way they behave when they are angry. At some point during their tantrum, they may feel shame for their behaviour, and this makes them even angrier. Now someone needs to be blamed, and of course, it is the child: "See how angry you have made me! Why do I have to shout at you like this before you listen? Why do you make me so upset? Do you enjoy seeing me like this?" These are just a few of the blame-shifters that parents use when they've lost their cool.

No matter how angry you feel, you are the adult in the situation, and it is up to you to behave like one. No matter who causes you to feel angry; whether it's your child or another adult or a situation, you have a choice whether you are going to stay in control or lose your cool. Nobody can *make* you angry. You choose to *get* angry. Another person cannot control your emotions through their behaviour. You are the only one who can control your emotions. So, the key lies within *you.* It is up to you to call upon your maturity and learn to control how you express your anger.

So, what do you do? How do you keep from losing your cool when you're facing a stubborn toddler or a teenager who is ignoring you?

Recognizing Your Triggers

One of the challenges of parenthood is that our kids seem to have a natural ability to find our buttons so that they can push them at the worst possible times. They seem to instinctively know when our patience is at its thinnest and our tolerance is at its lowest. And that's when they push our buttons. We explode and not only lose our temper, but also our dignity and a little bit of our child's respect and trust.

Feeling anger is normal. But we can do something about how we manage that feeling. If we can get angry without losing our temper, we can treat our children with the respect they deserve and behave with dignity ourselves.

The first and most crucial step to managing our behaviour when we are angry, ironically, is *not to* take any steps until we have calmed down. When you are angry, you are not reasonable. Everything is magnified and seems worse or more significant than it is. Your anger makes you want instant gratification. You want to teach your child a lesson then and there. But it's not really about the lesson you want to teach them, it's about making *you* feel better. And it never works.

Before you can control your anger, you need to be able to recognize it. Once you can do that, you will be able to put measures in place to prevent yourself from exploding. Try to recognize a pattern, and then you can change it. We've all experienced it—that moment before you let go and blow up. Usually, we wouldn't be aware of it because we'd be too busy yelling, but now that we are, it's worth a try to turn the camera speed down to slow motion and observe ourselves in those moments before we blow.

Where in your body do tension, stress, and anxiety live? Are you inclined to get a headache when you're stressed, or do you get a tightness in your belly? Maybe your stress lives in your neck and shoulders? Examine yourself and find out where your stress-point is—it will be the first place where you feel a physical reaction as your anger rises. If you're a head-person, you'll probably feel the blood rushing to your brain. If you're a tummy-person, you will feel the anger starting there. The point is, your body gives you a signal and it is possible to recognize that signal and do something about it before it's too late. It's called self-control.

As soon as your body gives you the signal, recognize it and have a plan of action. It may be taking a deep breath, counting backwards from ten to one, or even reciting a poem or a prayer in your head; whatever you choose, keep on doing it until you feel that you are calm and able to act in a reasonable, responsible way. Sometimes it's a good idea to share with your child when you feel that you are getting angry or even when you're merely feeling cranky. It won't hurt the image they have of you as a figure of authority it would probably make them respect you more. They will learn that it is human to feel cranky and get angry sometimes, and the example you set of how you handle it is something they will take with them into their adult lives.

A Few Techniques That Will Help You Keep Your Cool

Breathe: If you feel your body signalling that you're about to lose it, take a moment and breathe. A few deep breaths are sometimes all you need to restore your sanity and help you think clearly again.

Give yourself a time-out: Sometimes you need to give yourself a time-out rather than the child. It's completely okay to tell them that you can feel that you're getting angry and that you are going to take a time-out to get your feelings under control. Not only does it prevent a nasty and unnecessary fight, but it also sets an excellent example to them of how to behave when they feel themselves getting angry.

Don't react: You would do well to remember that just like you when you get angry, your child is not thinking clearly when they have lost their temper. They might fling accusations at you or even shout things like, "I hate you!" or "I wish I were never born!" We are all human. Words like these, especially when they come out of the mouths of our children, will hurt, and you might feel compelled to defend yourself or even lash out at them with some kind of retort. This is pointless and just adds fuel to the fire. The best thing to do is to remain calm yourself and not react at all. It takes two to tango, and they will find little satisfaction in picking a fight with someone who isn't reacting to them. Once they have spent their emotions, you could sit down and talk about what happened and discuss solutions for whatever the reason for their frustration was.

Tag out: If you have a partner, sometimes it's better to let them take over when you feel that you aren't getting anywhere or are going to lose control.

Take care of yourself: Parenting is hard work, especially in times where we have so many other pressures. Make sure that you have some "me-time", whether it's soaking in a bubble bath, playing a round of golf, or going to the library. It keeps you sane.

Forgive yourself: You will make mistakes. You will lose your cool. You are human.

2

DIGGING DEEPER INTO DISCIPLINE

Before we talk about positive discipline, it's important to gain a deeper understanding of discipline in general. We can all agree that the purpose of child discipline is so that a child may learn to behave in a manner that is appropriate and socially acceptable. But this is not the only reason why discipline is important. Without discipline, people would do whatever they wanted to without any regard for other people or the consequences of their actions. Discipline promotes positive behaviour and brings stability and structure to a person's life. That, in turn, contributes toward creating a healthier society and helps to make this old world a better place.

It is important to remember that discipline should be as much about the end result as it should be about the process of achieving that end result. You can make almost anybody do anything if you bully them hard enough. That is not what discipline should be like. The only unpleasant part of discipline should be the natural consequence of the negative behaviour if there is one. Discipline should teach. It should work with the mind to create a sense of responsibility and bring the understanding necessary to create permanent positive behaviour.

TYPES OF DISCIPLINE

It's generally agreed that there are five different types of child discipline, and while experts may not agree on which type is best, each is believed to have its merits. Your choice of discipline should be based on your temperament and the temperament of your child. It should take into consideration your culture and your family's beliefs about behaviour and discipline. Most people use a combination of discipline types rather than a single one since there isn't a specific type of discipline that works for all kids and families across the board.

It is good to keep in mind when choosing how you are going to discipline your child that you are not just teaching them a certain kind of behaviour, you are also consciously or subconsciously creating beliefs in their mind. Because children's minds work so very differently from adult minds and they are so easily influenced, we need to be very careful that we do not create false beliefs that will cause harm to their emotional health.

Let's take a look at the types of discipline as identified by the experts.

Positive Discipline

Positive discipline teaches children a value system that will stay with them throughout their lives. It is about guiding your child towards responsible behaviour and self-control rather than forcing them to obey an instruction or request simply because they are afraid of being punished. Positive discipline builds self-esteem and strengthens the development of self-control and self-motivation. Appropriate and persistent positive discipline teaches a child about consequences and taking responsibility for their actions. The ultimate goal is to encourage the child to learn how to manage their feelings and behaviour. A child that is in control is a positive, emotionally healthy, and happy child.

Gentle Discipline

Gentle discipline starts at birth and looks at the long term rather than just focusing on today's behaviour and addressing it. It teaches children how to make healthy decisions and how to express their feelings in socially appropriate ways. For example, a child who yells abuse at a sibling will not just get a time-out, he or she will also be taught that this is not an acceptable way to behave towards others and that they have a choice to use their words in kind ways. Gentle discipline also takes the feelings of the child seriously, and the parent will discuss the emotion that the child felt that caused them to yell at their sibling. The child will be allowed to give input toward solving the problem.

Other gentle discipline strategies include helping kids understand the underlying reasons for rules, teaching them about positive and negative consequences, and spelling out expectations ahead of time.

Boundary-Based Discipline

The theory behind boundary-based discipline is that children behave when they feel safe and have clear boundaries. Parents make the rules clear and explain the consequences upfront so that the child knows what to do and what will happen if they misbehave. Consequences are followed through and rules are consistently enforced. Children aren't allowed to "get away" with things.

Behaviour Modification

Behaviour modification is a bit like conditioning. Positive and negative consequences are used to encourage good behaviour and discourage bad behaviour. There would most likely be recurring positive consequences such as an agreement that the child gets half-an-hour game-time on the Playstation after they've finished their homework. The child will be reminded of this and praised if they comply. If they don't, they would simply not be allowed the game-time. Any protests would simply be ignored.

Emotion Coaching

Emotion coaching teaches kids about their feelings and that it's okay sometimes to feel the way they do. They learn how to deal with their emotions appropriately and how to put their feelings into words rather than act on them. Parents are required to be aware of, and to acknowledge, both their and their child's emotions. They are expected to validate the child's feelings and encourage them to verbalize how they feel. Emotion coaching also teaches children to understand and find their own solutions for their misbehaviour. For instance, a child who throws his toys when he gets angry or frustrated is encouraged to make a list of alternative things he can do to get rid of his frustration. He may list something like punching a pillow, doing frog-jumps, or even drawing an angry picture. When he gets angry or frustrated again, he is reminded of his list and encouraged to use one of his ideas to manage his feelings. Positive behaviour is encouraged with lots of praise and it is recommended that parents make a point of "catching their child being good" as often as possible.

COMMON DISCIPLINE TACTICS

If you did a survey and asked parents which part of parenting they like the least, discipline would probably be at the top of the list. Deep down we instinctively feel that discipline has to be something unpleasant. It is as if it has become a genetic part of the human thought process and the word conjures up images of angry adults and crying children. For many, the concept of discipline simply means that through making things unpleasant for the child, they will learn that their behaviour was unacceptable. This is then supposed to make them stop the behaviour to avoid the unpleasantness. Unfortunately, it doesn't always work that way, and when it does, it is always at a cost.

Let's take a look at some of the more common and sometimes old-fashioned techniques that are used to enforce discipline. Some of them may surprise you!

Time-out: This technique is said to be effective when it is clear precisely what the child has done wrong. It also works for you if you need a break from their behaviour. The child has to be at an age where they can understand the purpose of the punishment, so at least two years or older. The idea is that the child should be put in a boring place where it's quiet. Possibly a corner in the living room where you can keep an eye on them. Their bedroom is way too much fun and is a place where they should feel safe. It shouldn't be a place you go to to be punished. The bathroom is simply too dangerous. It is believed that time-outs work better with younger children because it makes them feel separated from their parent. This is similar to withholding affection because the child is being ignored. The child does not like this because it makes them feel lonely, unloved, and unsafe so they will behave differently in future to feel loved, significant and safe.

Physical punishment: Some parents still believe that a well-timed smack or a spanking is the way to go. Nowadays, in many countries, some laws prohibit parents from using corporal punishment. One of the reasons for this is that there is very little control over how violent physical punishment can become, especially if the parent is not in control of their temper. Things could quickly get out of hand and the child could be harmed physically. Physical punishment has also been proven to make kids more aggressive and teaches them that harming someone you love is okay.

Another form of punishment that constitutes physical punishment but is often seen as harmless is the infamous practice washing a child's mouth with soap or putting pepper or even chillies in their mouth. This punishment is often used on younger children for swearing or lying and can cause severe problems if the child happens to be allergic or chokes.

Taking away or threatening to take away privileges or items that the child values: This technique is often used for kids that are beyond the toddler-stage. Say, for example, your 10-year-old is dawdling with their homework, and you see that this is going to become a long session if you don't do something about it. You say: "If your homework isn't finished by half-past five, there will be no TV time for you tonight." Hopefully, the child will care enough about the TV time to get their homework done. Nowadays, kids own or have access to all sorts of electronic devices such as games, phones, music players, and more. They seem to be addicted to some of these devices, making it a handy disciplinary tool. The parent threatens to take away the device or access to it, and this is believed to be motivation enough for the child to change their mind about their behaviour.

Sending them to bed without their supper: Surprisingly enough, this form of punishment was quite common up until the early 2000s and is still employed by desperate parents sometimes. Access to food is easy for a parent to control and the general belief is that a child won't starve to death from missing one meal. The problem with this form of punishment, however, is that it seems rather cruel and does very little to modify the child's behaviour. They are thinking about the fact that they are hungry and not about what they did wrong. They are likely feeling rejected and unloved. If anything, punishment should at least focus the child's attention on what they did wrong.

Scaring kids with folklore into behaving: Some parents tell stories of monsters like the Boogeyman who will kidnap you and possibly even cook you and eat you if you stay out after dark, don't eat your food, or you don't want to go to sleep. Jack Frost will bite your toes if you don't wear your shoes. The evil witch, Baba Yaga, will take you to her house on a chicken foot, and even Santa Claus is used in many cultures to scare (or bribe?) kids into behaving well. Especially around Christmas time, parents can be heard issuing threats such as: "If you don't stop misbehaving, Santa isn't going to bring you any gifts this year."

Frightening kids into behaving with lies about monsters and villains seems cruel when you realize how real these creatures are to them. It also seems like the parent is subconsciously shifting the burden of disciplining the child to the imaginary creature to avoid doing it themselves.

Shaming and comparing: This tactic is widespread and many people think it is acceptable to use it to teach kids the difference between what they label as "good" and "bad" behaviour. Shaming usually involves a comment about what the child is. It gets into their character and gives the child a negative image about themselves. Shaming is used in a variety of situations and parents might say things like: "You're such a cry-baby!", "You're a very naughty girl!" "You're such a sissy!" "Why can't you be more like your cousin?" "Why are you so stupid?", and "Look at you! Nobody else is acting the way you are!"

There is a saying that goes: "Sticks and stones will break your bones, but words can never harm you." Nothing has ever been further from the truth. We all know that words can do much more harm than sticks and stones could ever dream of doing. Shaming may work in the short term for some kids, who will respond to being made to feel unworthy by trying extra hard to please their parents, but in the long term, many children will get tired of trying to achieve something that seems impossible and simply give up. The damage to their self-esteem is incalculable because their self-identity is shaped around what they hear about themselves. If they hear negative statements about themselves often enough, they will start to live them out and become what they are being called.

We are beginning to see that the "tried and trusted" methods of disciplining children may have been tried, but some of them can not be trusted. When we discipline our children, we have no intention of harming them in any way. Indeed, that is furthest from our minds. All we want is for them to learn appropriate behaviour and become healthy, balanced adults.

3

THE CORE OF POSITIVE DISCIPLINE

We've looked at the types, techniques, and common tactics of discipline. We've had a look at parenting styles, and we've seen how we thwart our efforts at disciplining our children. The time has come for us to dive in and take a more in-depth look into the reason you're reading this book - positive discipline. What is it? How does it work? How does it benefit your child? And most importantly, how do you do it?

UNDERSTANDING POSITIVE DISCIPLINE

The best way to understand what positive discipline is is to be very clear about what it is *not*. Positive discipline is *not* about punishment and taking away privileges or about handing out praise and rewards. These methods simply condition a child into behaving correctly in exchange for a reward or to avoid punishment.

Positive discipline promotes positive behaviour in kids through empathy, validation of their feelings, building relationships, and developing effective communication. One of the primary goals of positive discipline is to teach self-control and self-discipline. These two things become the internal force that drives our actions and our decisions. It is what causes us to behave well and perform responsibly even when there is no one to see. It is what gives us the desire to contribute to society positively because we feel capable, confident, and connected.

There Are No Bad Kids, Only Bad Behavior

Positive discipline teaches that there are no bad children, only bad behaviour. It shifts the focus from the child to the behaviour and addresses that. It will help you when you're standing in the grocery store, and your child is throwing a tantrum. It will help you when they won't eat their dinner or don't want to do their homework. It will help you solve many of those everyday problems that parents struggle with on a day-to-day basis.

Being a parent is a journey for the brave. It will exhilarate, frustrate, fascinate, exhaust, and inspire you. Guiding a tiny human from the first moments of their lives into adulthood is an enormous challenge and at times it can be overwhelming. We do the best we can for our kids. We try all sorts of methods, read books, take quizzes, and attend online seminars, only to be left with the feeling that we will never be able to do right by them.

Parenting doesn't come naturally to everybody, and that's okay. We can't all be Mary Poppins. But we can make an effort to learn how to do what is best for our kids. The most important thing we need to learn is to shift our focus from the immediate outcome that we desire to the long-term effect that discipline (and punishment) has on our kids.

Discipline should be about teaching them to choose to do the right thing for the right reason. Being afraid of a slap is not the right reason for choosing to obey an instruction. Our actions when we discipline our children contribute primarily to their perception of discipline, decency, and obedience and influences who they will become as teenagers and adults.

You will hear parents say they feel tired, guilty, and emotionally drained daily from continually having to nag, beg, coax, lecture and yell to get things done. Sometimes they will express the wish that there was a different way because it makes them feel disconnected from their children when they are continually butting heads with them.

Well, their wish has been granted. There IS a different way.

Positive discipline begins at birth and lasts a lifetime. It is kind but firm. It is nonviolent and respectful. It focuses on encouragement and problem-solving and teaches children valuable social and life skills. It builds character and teaches kids to make informed choices, and most importantly, it is effective in the long term.

One of the reasons positive discipline works is that it focuses on the *behaviour* of the child and not on the child. When we discipline our kids, we tend to get into their character without even realizing what we are doing. This is because we are focusing on the child and not on what they have done or are busy doing.

When we tell them *they're* being naughty, we're putting a label on *them*. When we say that their *behaviour* is naughty, we are putting the label on the *behaviour*, separating the child from the behaviour and enabling them to look at it objectively. This makes it easier for them to come up with solutions to change or modify their behaviour because they do not see it as changing themselves, they are just changing something they do, and that is a lot less daunting.

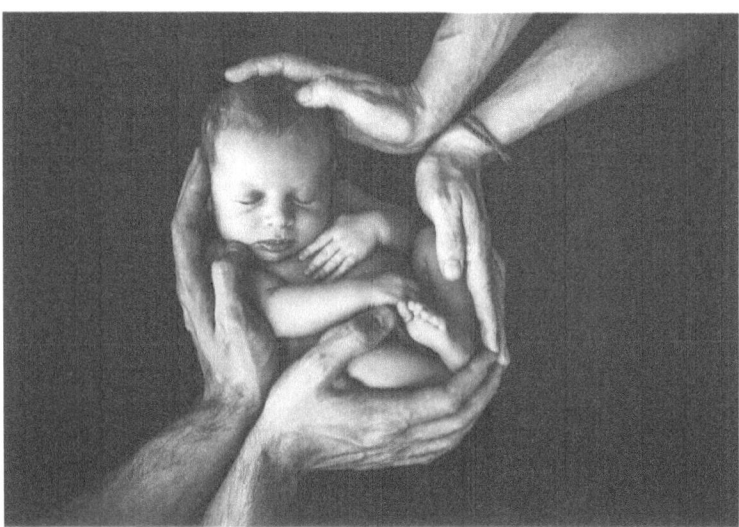

Parenting Goals

We can also say that positive discipline is a set of principles that can be applied to guide all of your interactions with your children. It is an approach to discipline that looks at both the short-term and the long-term goals of parenting. What do we mean by this?

Short-term parenting goals: These are the things that you wish to accomplish daily. For example, you would like your daughter to be ready to leave for school on time in the morning because if she is late, it causes you to be late for work, and she tends to dawdle. This sounds like a single goal, but it isn't. Let's break it up into all the things that she needs to do to achieve this goal: She has to get up when you wake her, make her bed, get dressed, have her breakfast, brush her teeth, pack her school bag, and get in the car so that you can leave, drop her off at school, and be on time for work. That's a whole list of short-term goals right there.

In another example, Jonathan needs to stop teasing his sister *right now* so that she can stop crying and you can have peace and quiet, or, Jane needs to get off the street and on the pavement *right now* so that she can be safe from oncoming traffic.

So, short-term parenting goals are all the things you want to achieve *right now* (or at least as soon as possible) so that life can keep on happening. As you can see, the list of short-term goals is never-ending. That's because every day is jam-packed with right-now-moments that frequently create short-term goals.

This constant bombardment of short-term goals causes us to lose sight of where we should be going. We solve one problem most quickly and easily we can think of so that we can move on to the next one, too busy to stop for a moment to think where the journey is taking us. What is the real purpose of what we are doing? How is getting your daughter ready for school on time and making Jonathan stop teasing his sister going to give them a better future? How is it going to build character and teach them to make better choices?

Long-term parenting goals: Your long-term goals are the real reason why you should be disciplining your kids. Achieving short-term parenting goals provides you with the instant gratification of having your immediate needs met, but your long-term parenting goals are what you want your child to achieve by the time they've grown up.

While short-term parenting goals are often about an end-result that *you* want, long-term parenting goals should not be about you, or what you want. It should be about the human in your care for whose future you've taken responsibility. It should be about teaching your child about love, morality, integrity, responsibility, honesty, resilience, decision-making, and so much more. It is about making sure that they go into their future, fully equipped, confident, and happy.

THE PRINCIPLES AND PRACTICES OF POSITIVE DISCIPLINE

Positive discipline is based on mutual respect. Often parenting advice focuses on the need of the adult to get the child to behave and not on the needs of the child. That kind of discipline doesn't promote mutual respect. It creates merely feelings of submission, rebellion, and fear.

Be Kind, But Firm

Positive discipline requires you to be kind and firm at the same time. Maintaining the balance isn't easy, and some parents tend to emphasize being firm over being kind, while others will let their kindness take them to the point of passivity. In some relationships, one parent may be strict, and the other parent may lean towards lenience and a relaxed attitude to discipline.

It is essential that this imbalance is corrected and that both parents learn how to be firm and kind at the same time. A situation like the above can quickly get out of hand because the lenient parent will try to be even more relaxed to make up for the parent whom they feel is being too rigid, and the strict parent will tighten the reins to make up for the lenient parent. It becomes a situation where parents are battling each other, each believing that they are doing right by the child, and the poor child is left confused and frustrated because they never know whether they are doing right or wrong.

Other parents may be lenient to a point where their kids have gotten entirely out of hand, then, when they come to the realization that they are raising ungrateful, entitled, children, they suddenly turn it all around and become so strict that they are frequently in combat with the children that they were spoiling not so long ago.

Being kind doesn't always mean being nice, and being firm doesn't mean that you have to be nasty. We make many mistakes in the name of kindness because we don't completely understand the meaning. We are not kind to our children when we're continually rescuing them and over-protecting them. Sometimes they have to struggle or suffer a bit to make them stronger. They need to understand that they cannot always have what they want and that life doesn't always go the way you'd like it to. Of course, you should not purposefully cause them to suffer, but sometimes you have to allow them to suffer or struggle and simply give them your love and support.

Let's say for example that your little boy is upset and crying because he wants a toy that he sees while you're grocery shopping and you've told him to put it back on the shelf. Now you have a choice. You could say something like: "You know you can't always have what you want. Stop your crying! You're behaving like a spoiled brat."

Or, you could use the "kind but firm" approach and say: "It can be very disappointing when we can't have what we want and I can see that you are upset right now. Remember, I love you."

And then you stop talking and carry on shopping even if he keeps on crying (which he probably will do for a while until he realizes that it is not getting him anywhere). You've acknowledged and validated his feelings. You didn't change your mind about the toy (you were firm), and you reminded him that you love him (you are giving him love and support without rescuing him). He will learn that he is capable of surviving the little ups and downs of life, and this develops resilience.

Your teenage daughter might not have done so well on her last test, and she is upset. You know that she didn't do her very best to prepare, so she probably deserves it, but that's not what you say. All you say is this: "I can see you're disappointed that you didn't do as well as you would have liked." Then hug her and don't say anything. That's the hard part. No rescuing, no explanations, just loving support. She will discover on her own that she can get over her disappointment and she'll probably admit to herself that she would have done better if she'd worked harder and do better next time.

Choose a Strategy and Stick to It

One of the problems we have with controlling the behaviour of others is that we can't! Positive discipline recognizes that, but it also recognizes that your behaviour can influence how another person behaves. You may find that you're often frustrated because your child will not behave the way you want them to, but have you considered the possibility that changing your behaviour could change theirs? It's a lot easier deciding what you are going to do than it is forcing your child to do what you want them to do.

The most important part of this technique is that you have to follow through on your decision. If your actions do not agree with your words, all you will end up with is frustration and a confused child.

Let's see how it works:

- Your toddler makes changing very difficult because they wiggle and jump around, making it virtually impossible for you to get their clothes on. Rather than continue the daily struggle, you tell the child: "I can't dress you without your help, so I'm going to wait here until you're ready to stand still and help me with this." The first time could take a while, and you will have to exercise some patience, but the child will soon realize that putting up a fight when getting dressed is not fun when nobody is fighting back. As soon as they stop their wiggling, you carry on dressing them. If they start jumping around again, you stop. It will take a few times for them to understand that this is how changing is going to be from now on, but if you stick to your guns, they will start cooperating with you.
- Sometimes we don't realize that we are "talking our kids deaf". By continually repeating what we said, we teach our kids that they don't have to listen the first

time around. If you find that you have to say everything twice because they either didn't hear you or claim to have not understood, next time, make sure that you have their full attention when you speak to them. You can do this by asking them to look at you while you are talking and letting them repeat back to you what you said in their own words—this ensures that they understood what you said. Allow them to ask questions and make sure that they know that you are not going to repeat yourself. And then don't. Stick to your guns, and you will find that your kids will listen much better when you are talking to them.

- Sometimes kids will have a habit of leaving things to the last minute, and then they spring them on you. They tell you at nine o'clock in the evening that they need muffins for the class or that they need help with a project that is due tomorrow. Let them know that you are available to help them with their projects and tasks *before* a specific time in the evening, but not after. When the child comes to you after the agreed time, simply remind them that you were available until that time, but now you have other things to do. You are sorry, but they are on their own on this one. Be kind, but firm. This is not the time to feel sorry for them and give them another chance after a lecture. Even if they get angry and throw accusations at you, stick to your guns and allow them to suffer the consequences of their actions. Remember, *don't lecture*, and *don't give in*. You are allowing them to learn from their behaviour, and this is the kind of lesson that sticks.

We have learnt that being kind but firm takes a lot of courage and following through from you as a parent, but that it has wonderful long-term rewards that make it worth it.

Act More—Talk Less

When was the last time that you actively listened to yourself when you're interacting with your kids? Take a day to intentionally listen to yourself and to other parents that you come across. Hear yourself bargaining with your child to get them to eat their breakfast, listen to how you nag them to get their teeth brushed, take note of how you frequently explain why they should do this or that, and finally, notice how many times you say, "Do this" and "Don't do that."

Younger children have a short attention span, and we tend to drown them in our constant stream of words. They hear the first few words we say, and then they tune out. If you know your child, and you are aware, you will be able to see at which point their eyes glaze over, and your words have just become a stream of noise. Because when they hear, "Do this, do that" hundreds of times a day, they tune that out too, and when they don't react to us, we label them as disobedient. So how do we stop talking and start acting?

- Your toddler is throwing a tantrum because they don't want to go to bed. They want to keep on playing with her toys. It's quite in order to pick them up and carry them to their bedroom and put them in their bed or to firmly take them by the hand and start walking them in the direction you want them to go. Say nothing, simply act. Shouting, begging, threatening, or ordering your child is disrespectful and simply adds fuel to the fire.
- If kids are fighting over a toy, simply take it away from them and put it where they can see it but they can't reach it. There is no need to explain to them that they can have it back when they stop fighting over it. Your actions send the message clearer than words.
- Sometimes you do need a few words to get the message across but keep it short. If your child tends to dawdle in the public bathrooms at the mall, rather than give her a long speech about why you want her to get done and get it over with, simply talk her through the process by saying something like: "Enough chatter for now. Get done. Wipe. Flush. Wash hands. Let's go."
- In our efforts to be polite and respectful to our kids, we sometimes overdo it by asking them to do the things that we know they need to do rather than merely reminding them. We ask questions like, "Don't you think you should make your bed now?" or, "Would you like to have your bath now?" and then we are surprised when the child honestly responds that they

do not think they should make their bed and they most certainly would not like to have their bath now.

It is just as respectful to simply use a few words to remind or inform the child of what you need them to do. When you get into the car, you could simply say, "It's time to put seatbelts on." At supper time, simply tell them, "It's supper time." If they are old enough to make their bed, you can remind them by saying, "We make our beds before we leave the house in the morning." When you use short, simple statements rather than lengthy explanations or questions, there is nothing left to discuss or argue about. Because you are confident and clear and leave nothing to debate, kids will accept that that is how it works and comply.

Follow Through All the Way

All children have specific behaviour patterns that drive us up the walls. A favourite for little ones is distracting you while you're on the phone, and some will even go as far as trying to take it away from you. They do this for a variety of reasons ranging from wanting to say hello to the person you're talking to, to simply being jealous of the fact that someone else is getting your full attention. Or your kids could be fighting in the car every single time you go somewhere, and it's driving you to the point where you wish you could just put them in the trunk. So how does following through help us here?

There is no point in planning a strategy in the heat of the battle, so you need to address the behaviour before it happens again. Find an appropriate time when you can give your child your full attention, then sit them down and talk with them to try and find out what it is that they want when they behave the way that they do. Whatever their reasons, acknowledge their feelings and agree with them that it would be wonderful for them to have it their way if that were possible. There is no need to explain why it is not.

Involve them in finding a solution by allowing them to make suggestions and agree together on what they are going to do about their behaviour. Tell them what you are going to do if they repeat it. Make sure that they understand that you are not going to allow their behaviour to continue and set your limit. Also, make sure that whatever you say you are going to do if the behaviour repeats itself is something that you are willing and able to follow through on.

There is no point in saying that you will turn around and go home if there is a fight in the car again unless you are 100 percent sure that you can do that. Sometimes it's necessary to be creative with your solutions, but it's worth it. Your child learns that there are boundaries that have to be respected; they learn how to find solutions, and they learn that they can depend on you to keep your word.

. . .

Turn Mistakes Into Opportunities

We know by now that positive discipline does not use punishment. We agree that fear should not be the motivation for doing the right thing. Punishment is unpleasant, makes everyone feel bad, and research has proven that it is not a very effective way to achieve positive outcomes. Parents use punishment because it gives them a sense of being in control. But does it? Have you noticed that you are punishing the same behaviour over and over again?

Positive discipline requires parents to become actively involved in helping their child find solutions to problems and teach them how to manage situations appropriately. Let's take a look at a few examples to see how we do this:

- Your toddler has tipped over his milk because he wasn't sitting still as you asked. Rather than shout at him that it wouldn't have happened if he'd listened, you grab a cloth for each of you and say: "You see why it's a good idea to sit still when we drink milk? Let's quickly clean this up together." Without accusing him, you remind him that it was his actions that caused the spill and you involve him by letting him help you clean up the mess.
- Your teenager has neglected to do her chores on time. If you scold her or take away her phone, the chores still won't get done on time, and she will learn nothing. Go

to her and remind her that it's time to do her chores. If she tries to get away with an excuse to do it later, firmly remind her that you had an agreement with her that the chores would be done by a particular time and you would like her to keep it. You are teaching her responsibility and integrity.

- Your little one is playing with the cat, but the game is getting rough, and you fear that one of the two will get hurt. Rather than yell at the little one to leave the cat alone, take the cat away and tell the child that they can play with the cat again when they are ready to play more gently.
- Toddlers and babies sometimes hit us or pull our hair. Many people believe that you should do the same back to them so that they can feel what it feels like, and then they will stop. This doesn't work—all they learn is to hurt somebody back when they are hurt. Instead, take their hand and show them how to be gentle - pat yourself with their hand and say, "Touch gently."

Give Them a Choice

You don't have to be smart or highly educated to be a good decision-maker. All you need is common sense, and giving options with limits teaches kids common sense by allowing them to make a choice and then either suffer or enjoy the consequences depending on the choice they made.

Children who aren't allowed to make choices will become dependent adults who rely on others to make their decisions for them. Your ability to make sensible informed choices puts you in charge of your own life.

- Either/or choices work best for younger kids. Give them simple choices, such as whether they want spinach or beans or whether they want to have their snack before or after doing their homework. You can also give choices like, "Do you want me to help you with your shoes or do you want to put them on yourself?"
- Kids get older, and their choices get more complicated. Your daughter wants to quit tennis, but it's important to you that she takes part in at least one physical activity. There's no point in forcing her to do something that she doesn't enjoy, so you say: "I'm quite happy for you to quit playing tennis, but I need you to choose another physical activity instead. What would you like to try?"
- Choices can help a child learn about consequences. Your son has spent 30 minutes studying for an important test, and he says he's done. You say: "I know you like to do well on your tests and another half an hour or so could make a difference, but it's up to you whether you want to put in that extra half an hour or not."

- When you offer that choice, you must be sure that you are comfortable with the idea that he might fail the test or do poorly. If you aren't, don't offer the choice. If he chooses not to study the extra half an hour, and he fails or does poorly, he will learn through experience that the other option was the better one. If he chooses to study the extra half hour and he does well, this positive experience teaches him that the responsible choice was the better one.

The examples above all have one thing in common. You are offering choices that are acceptable to you, and the child is choosing the one that they are happiest with. There is no power struggle because you are not giving an ultimatum; you are giving a choice. The child feels a sense of control which in turn builds self-esteem.

4

A DIFFERENT APPROACH

When we think about discipline, we need to remember that it's not a "one size fits all" thing. What works for your son will probably not work for your daughter. What works for your teenager will not work for your toddler. It's not just the age of the child that matters; their personality also has an influence. It makes sense that a timid toddler would most likely respond to yelling by starting to cry and doing as they're told, while a more confident or cheeky one might even yell back and refuse even more vehemently to comply. We are not always aware of what our kids are capable of understanding at a given age. Sometimes we overestimate them, and sometimes we underestimate them.

In this section, we will look at the ages and stages of development of kids and what level of understanding they have of our expectations of them. We will also look at effective ways to discipline them what consequences they can understand and learn from.

While children don't develop and progress at the same speed and they most certainly don't all behave in the same way, it is possible to group more or less at what level their communication skills and understanding should be at a certain age as well as their physical abilities. The emphasis here should be on "more or less" because no child will fit precisely into any parameters set by science.

However, suppose you notice that your child's behaviour or level of understanding falls way beyond these parameters. In that case, you should consider that they may be facing a challenge that requires that you seek guidance from a professional. Here are some things to look out for:

- Prolonged development of speech and motor skills could indicate possible brain damage or developmental delays - brain damage can occur for a wide variety of reasons and is not always picked up at birth. There are myriad reasons for developmental delays.
- If your child is always all over the place, struggles to focus for even a short period of time, is easily frustrated, behaves impulsively and has very little self-control, the problem could be that they have attention deficit hyperactivity disorder (ADHD).
- A child with autism would show symptoms such as

avoiding eye contact and not responding when you say their name. They don't return your smile. If they talk, they might repeat the same phrase over and over again. They show little interest in their siblings or even you. They might get very upset and throw terrible tantrums when they don't like something, and they tend to display repetitive movements such as rocking or flapping their hands.

If you notice these or any other patterns of behaviour, you must seek the help of a health professional as soon as possible. There is a lot of support for people with kids who have challenges, and both you and your child will benefit.

AGES, STAGES, AND DISCIPLINE

Positive discipline begins at birth and continues throughout your relationship with your child. That's because positive discipline isn't just a tool you use on your child. It becomes a way of thinking that is helpful in almost every situation where there is the possibility of conflict or disagreement.

Welcome, Tiny Earthling!

Think of your baby as a small, helpless, dependent little being that has just emerged from the cosy, quiet warmth of the womb into a bright, noisy, scary world. Inside the womb, his needs were automatically met, and he was never cold or hungry. Now, this little being is utterly dependent on you to satisfy his hunger, clean him when he has soiled himself, and most importantly, to give him the sense of security that he had inside the womb. This is why the first few months of your baby's life are critical. This is when you establish your first bond with your child. Babies don't have words to say what they want. They cry when they want us to know that they need something because that is their only means of communication.

The best you can do during this stage is to be there for them and show them that they are safe. They need to be held, cuddled, rocked and carried, and their needs have to be met consistently. They need to know that they can rely on you. Establishing this trust in infancy will make your baby more likely to accept limits later on, and they won't be afraid to learn new things because they know that they can trust you to take care of them.

Sometimes we take a little too long to respond to our baby's cries, and they become more frantic. We tend to say the baby is getting angry. Babies do not yet know what anger is. The only emotion they understand is need. They are crying because they have a need that isn't being fulfilled, and their instinct is to cry louder and more urgently to get your attention.

A baby will cry even though it has been fed, it's nappy is dry and as far as you can see, it should be comfortable. When this happens, people say the baby is naughty and should be left to "cry it out." At that young age, a baby doesn't know how to be naughty. Your child is probably just in need of love and reassurance. Pick them up and give them the love and reassurance they need. It's a small sacrifice to make for the health and welfare of your child. Letting them cry it out just causes undue stress to the whole family.

Babies will grab objects such as your glasses or jewellery or pull your hair—they will grab at anything they can reach and try to put it in their mouth. All you have to do is gently take the object away from them or disentangle their hand from your hair.

Some people believe that you should smack their hand to teach them not to grab at things. This makes no sense because they are merely acting on their instinct, and they aren't aware of what they are doing. The pain and suddenness of a smack will make them let go of what they are holding onto, but they will not understand why you have hurt them, and they will lose a little bit of their trust in you. You have just demonstrated to them that it's okay to hurt someone that you love. It is your job to protect them, not hurt them.

Still Becoming Human

As they enter into the second half of their first year on Earth, your little one will steal your heart with beaming smiles and break it with the passion of their tears. This is a hard time for little ones. They are ready to explore a grand, new world, but only if there's someone by their side. They are much more aware of you and tend to cry when you leave the room. No matter how many times you come back, in the mind of a child this age, when they can't see you, you are gone, and they feel lonely and helpless.

This is also the time that most babies begin teething, and this is one of the most painful and uncomfortable processes they will ever have to go through. Most little ones suffer from fever and diarrhoea, and their gums constantly itch or hurt. Being so young, they have no idea what is going on, and all they can do is depend on you to do what you can to help them through it with love and compassion.

There is one more interesting reason why babies cry when they are this age. You will find that this kind of crying usually happens around the same time each day or night. This is part of the process of their body and their brain, developing a rhythm and an essential part of their growth. Just comfort your child. Hold them and make them feel loved.

Crying isn't the only thing a baby between the ages of six and twelve months old does. They do other things that are way more fun and exciting, such as sitting up by themselves and saying their first words. Yes, this is when they start communicating. Responding to your child's babbling teaches them that the sounds they are making are important, and they will practice them. In the beginning, they just babble away, but one magical day they will smile at you angelically and say, "mama" or "dada" as if they mean it and your heart will explode.

The Young Explorer

Between the ages of one and two years old, a child develops at an incredible speed. This period is a journey of discovery as they go from sitting and crawling to standing up against things and walking by themselves. Suddenly the world is so much bigger, and their new mobility puts them in reach of so many new things!

Your child becomes an explorer and a scientist. He has loads of questions that need answers: What do things feel like? What do they taste like? What sound will they make when they fall? What will happen if you bang them together? Will they float in the bath? Will they disappear if you throw them in the toilet? The list is endless, and it's your job to make sure that your young explorer is safe while he experiments and inspects his world.

A child of this age does not know the difference between what they are allowed to do and what not to do, and they don't know what the result of their action is going to be. Rather than put your child in danger or end up jumping around like a ninja to save things from falling, think safety over aesthetics in your home. Put away objects and ornaments that can harm your child. Put pot plants out of reach. Move furniture with sharp edges and corners to a safe spot. In short, make sure that your child cannot hurt themselves in that one moment that you aren't watching them—that's how long it takes for an accident to happen.

Your child's vocabulary is exploding and now is an excellent time to enjoy exploring with them while you teach them the names of objects and explain what is happening to them. Give your child a chance to speak. Listen to them and try to answer their questions as simply as you can. Make them feel important, help them learn, and nurture their growing independence.

Remember that though they can name objects, they don't know the words for their feelings yet. Their favourite word is "no", and they use it to tell you that they don't like something, they don't want to wear that jacket, they're frustrated, they're hungry, and loads of other things. Rather than see it as defiance, try to understand that it's them trying to tell you how they feel with their limited vocabulary.

On the other side of the coin, it is important to know that your toddler is not yet capable of understanding that you have needs and feelings too, so they are not selfish when they disregard the fact that you need a few moments of peace and quiet and insist on your attention or make a noise.

There is no point in trying to discipline your child at this age. They are too young to understand commands and if you say "no", they will probably just say it back to you. A useful tactic is to distract them or make a game of what you want them to do.

The Frightened Little Tyrant

Sometimes this stage is called the terrible twos, but it doesn't have to be. All it takes is a compassionate understanding of the way your child views the world right now and respecting their feelings. Between the age of two and three years old your child goes through some radical changes that you might even find concerning, but there is no need for concern—they are just learning about the world and developing into little individuals.

Out of the blue, your child suddenly becomes clingy and fearful. They're afraid of all sorts of things that they never took notice of before. They become clingy and cry when you leave them. They're afraid of the dark, the neighbour's dog, and the shadow in the corner. Movie characters, cartoon characters, toys, masks, and imaginary creatures terrify them. What happened?

This is because their imagination is developing, and everything is real and alive to them. If they believe that the creature in a cartoon can get out of the book and eat them, it is as real to them as getting up in the morning and brushing your teeth is to you.

While their imagination is growing, they are also becoming aware that bad things can happen to them. They need your reassurance and support whether the threat is real or imaginary. The worst thing you can do is laugh off their fears and tell them they're silly.

Along with their imagination, their awareness of danger is also developing. Your previously outgoing toddler suddenly becomes shy around strangers and hides behind your legs or turns their face away when they try to talk to them. Your toddler isn't being rude. They just don't feel comfortable with someone that they don't know, because they are becoming aware of danger.

Your toddler knows Auntie Jane quite well, why are they refusing to let their aunt pick them up onto her lap? Once again, they're not rude. They just want control over their own body and to choose by whom and when they are picked up.

During this time, your child will sometimes behave like a narcissist with bipolar disorder. They will move between extremes of aggression and withdrawal, and they will be bossy, possessive, jealous, self-centred, and rigid.

Even small changes are very hard for them and they like repetition, so using routines where you can will make things easier for everybody. Make sure bedtime is at the same time every evening and establish a ritual such as a story or a song when they're all tucked in. Talk with them while you do what you need to so that they are already doing what you want before they get a chance to think it over and resist.

They have only one concept of time, and that is "now" and their own needs and desires are most important to them right now, so don't expect them to wait for things or be willing to share easily patiently. There is not much scope for disciplining your child during this stage. Your best tactic is prevention and distraction. Whispering when you tell them something works because it's fun for them and gets their attention. Praise for things done well also goes a long way.

The Student Quizmaster

Between the ages of three and five years, your child will grow from an insecure little tyrant into an energetic, curious, entertaining little creature who will both enchant and exasperate you. As they emerge from their fears and become more secure, and as their language capability develops, they have more and more questions. They want to know what things are called, how they work, and a myriad of other things. They also know why they have to brush their teeth, put on their clothes, and eat their dinner. When they ask, "Why?" they really want to know. Some parents think that the child is defiant when they want to know why they have to brush their teeth, and the child is told, "Because I said so." From your point of view, they are questioning an instruction, but from their point of view, they are looking for information. If they know the reason why they are brushing their teeth, they are more likely to do it.

This is also the stage where kids need to begin to learn about rules, and just like brushing their teeth, they are much more likely to follow the rules if they understand the reasons for them. Your rules should mainly be to keep them safe and you shouldn't have too many. You could have a rule that they should always hold your hand when you're walking in town. Praise your child when they remember a rule and if they break it, explain to them again why the rule exists. And finally, let them play. The more they play, the better. It is very important for their development and teaches them problem-solving skills and builds confidence.

The Fledgeling

Most kids go to some school around the age of five, and for both the child and the parents, this is a significant event. How you manage this will have a considerable influence on how your child handles it. If you are afraid that they're going to be scared and insecure, you will transfer these feelings to them. Be introspective. Are you maybe the one that is afraid of letting go? You might be afraid that something could happen to your child while they are not under your care. These fears transfer to your child and make them feel insecure and afraid. If you prepare them for their first school day and show them that you have confidence in them, they will likely reflect that confidence and make the transition quite smoothly.

Your child must now learn how to get along with a larger group of new children all at once, and they have a teacher whose attention they have to share with lots of other kids, there are new routines and a whole lot of new rules. This is a whole new world that exists outside the home, and this is where the foundations you laid, in the beginning, will begin to show.

The next five years will have their ups and downs, and both you and your child will go through a lot together. They will go through periods where they are rebellious and seem angry at the whole world, and there will be times when they're so angelic, you're sure you can see a tiny halo floating above their heads!

During this time, they will begin to develop friendships and even make an enemy or two! Your child is becoming socially aware and is learning about how others behave, think, and believe. Continue to build on the foundations of kindness and respect that you laid from birth as you guide them through these crucial years.

By the time your child is ten, they will have a good sense of when they are doing things that they're not supposed to be doing or if they are telling a lie. You can now begin to involve them by calling on their ability to tell right from wrong. Talk to them about what they did and help them to evaluate their behaviour by asking questions like,

"What were you hoping would happen when you did what you did?"

"Was there a little voice in your heart that said, "Don't do it?"

"What made you decide to ignore the little voice?"

"What else could you have done?"

Listen to your child's answers, acknowledge their feelings, and keep asking questions until you have guided your child toward figuring out how they could have handled whatever the problem had been.

Flying Practice

The stage between 10 and 13 years of age is also called the "tweens". This is because your child is hovering between being a child and being a teenager. Their behaviour will be surprisingly mature at times, but most of the time, they will behave like the children that they still are. It can be a confusing time for your child. Their body is preparing for adulthood, and the physical changes are accompanied by hormonal imbalances that can cause moodiness and even make them feel depressed.

They are becoming more and more aware of their individuality; they are noticing that they don't always agree with their parents and that people have different beliefs. They start to become more independent, and friends become very important.

Your child is at an age where you can reason with them and rather than bully them into doing what you want them to. You could say something like this to a child who keeps postponing their homework and then rushes it off in the morning before school: "It seems like it puts a lot of pressure on you when you have to rush like that, and there's no time to check for mistakes, is there? Let's see how we can go about it so that your homework is done before you go to sleep at night."

Up, Up, and Away!

At the age of 14, your child is a young adolescent, and with every passing year, they will grow a little more into becoming the responsible, happy, balanced adults we set out for them to become. Even though your child still lives at home, they slowly start "leaving the nest." You see them less frequently as they become more and more involved with school activities and friends.

The lessons your child has learnt will begin to show—this is what you've been practising for. Because you have always treated them with respect, your child has learnt to respect others; they will be able to resolve conflict, communicate their feelings, make good choices, and stand up for themselves and others. Of course, there will be challenges. They are not fully grown up yet, but the foundation that has been laid will allow them to weather the storms of failure and carry them through the challenges that life brings.

5

GUIDING YOUR CHILD'S BEHAVIOR

I was going to name this chapter "Managing Your Child's Behavior" because that's a familiar term and it's used by most experts when they talk about working with your child's behaviour. But, as I progressed with my writing, I began to feel uncomfortable. I kept feeling as if the child's behaviour was some kind of entity that has to be managed. Talking about managing made it feel as if the behaviour was detached from the person. After much thinking, I concluded that we *guide* our child's behaviour when we use positive discipline, we do not manage it. Our child's behaviour isn't a "something" that needs managing. Our child is a little person, and their behaviour needs to be guided so that they may learn to make the right choices.

Why did I go out of my way to find a different word and not just go with the one the experts have been using? Does it matter what you call it if you are doing it right? Yes, it does. This is not a case of, "a rose by any other name smells just as sweet." It is essential, and here's why:

As we learn to talk, read, and write, we become conditioned to understand that certain words or concepts have a specific meaning. We later learn that many of these words have more than one meaning, but our first impression of the word is usually the one that sticks. This is usually also the most common meaning of the word, and if you're aware, you might even notice that you have a mental image that pops up briefly when you say or think of certain words.

What Does Managing Really Mean?

Say the word "manager" out loud. What image popped into your mind when you heard yourself say it? Depending on who you are, it could be an image of your boss or a manager at a business or store. They are most likely giving instructions and making sure everything is happening as it should when it should.

Our brain is a strange and wonderful thing, and it sometimes makes exciting connections. When you say or think that you are managing your child's behaviour, your brain takes the word "manage" and conjures up the image of the manager. You start behaving according to your interpretation of what "managing" means. You give the child instructions and make sure they know what to do and when they need to do it. You apply disciplinary techniques and come up with new strategies. You plan and instruct, and run their lives like a well-oiled machine. And the moment you stop, so do they, and it all falls into chaos. Why?

According to the Mirriam-Webster dictionary, the word "manage" means: "to make and keep compliant," and when most people manage, this is precisely what they are doing. Most people's understanding of managing is that it is an ongoing thing. If the manager of a business or store does not do their job and manage the staff and processes, the business will fall into chaos and fail.

When you look up the meaning of "to make and keep compliant," you will find that it is saying that you should first make something (or someone) conform to specific requirements, and then you should consistently keep on making them conform to those requirements.

In our efforts to make and keep our kids compliant, we continuously repeat ourselves, give instructions, remind, supervise, and check. We think we are "managing" their behaviour, but we are just programming them. We are continually supervising them and telling them what to do so they learn to wait for instructions or approval. As soon as there is no one to monitor, approve and remind them continuously, they feel insecure, and then they start misbehaving and forget what they're supposed to do.

. . .

Why Is Guiding Better?

The word "guiding" can conjure up a wide variety of images. One person might imagine someone helping a blind person cross the street, and another might imagine a mountain guide showing them the way up Mount Everest. No matter what image comes up in your mind, you will find that in some or other way, guiding means pointing someone in the right direction and consistently nudging them in that direction until they are there.

When we are guiding our kids' behaviour, we are not pushing or forcing them to do things out of habit, or as a result of being prompted or reminded, or out of fear of punishment. A child who is guided wisely learns to behave responsibly and make good choices.

Shifting the Focus

Positive discipline teaches that there are no bad kids; there is just bad behaviour. The first thing we have to do is learn to shift our focus from our child to their behaviour. The most effective way to do this is to change the words we use when we describe what they are doing. Your child isn't what they do. Your child isn't naughty. They are displaying naughty behaviour. Your child isn't rude. The behaviour they are displaying is rude.

When we are guiding our child's behaviour or disciplining them, it is important to remember that *two* people are interacting. Discipline as not a one-way process, and it is not something you are doing *to* your child. It's something you are doing *with* your child. *Both* of you are doing something. Your child's behaviour triggered a response or reaction from you, and your response triggered a response or reaction in them. What your child will learn depends on how you responded to them.

When we lose our temper, we might say to our child: "See how angry you've made me?" Your child cannot *make* you angry. You *decide* to become angry. We saw in the first chapter that there is a moment that passes before we lose our temper, and if we can identify that moment, we can change how we respond to a situation.

The only person that can control your behaviour and is *you*. This applies from the first moment you are born until you breathe your last breath on earth. Everything you do is because of a conscious or subconscious choice that you are making. *Nobody* can *make* you do anything, and that goes for every single person on this planet, including your child! It is called free will, and we all have it. Your job as a parent or caregiver is to teach your child to use their free will to make conscious, positive choices.

POSITIVE ATTENTION = POSITIVE BEHAVIOR

If something isn't bothering you, you tend to ignore it and leave it alone. Many of us unknowingly do the same with our kids. When they are behaving well, we hardly notice them, but as soon as they misbehave, we're all over them. If misbehaving is the only way to get the attention they need, it makes sense that this is what kids will do when they feel neglected, lonely, or simply want your attention.

Most people are very good at catching their kids at bad behaviour, but how good are you at catching your child at being good? Kids who get enough positive attention don't have a need to misbehave to get attention, but how do you give your child positive attention, and how do you catch your child being good?

Giving Your Child Positive Attention

One way to give your child positive attention is to play with them. Attend your toddler's "tea party" with their dolls and teddies; help them build a tower with blocks or draw a picture together. Pick a time where you won't be interrupted and make sure those few minutes belong exclusively to you and your child. While you are playing, avoid giving instructions and asking loads of questions. Instead, focus on what the child is doing and praise them when you can. You could comment on how beautifully they have arranged the teacups or how hard they are working at stacking blocks to make their tower, or how carefully they are colouring within the lines. Whatever you say, make sure your comments are honest and sincere, and whatever you do, make sure you both have fun. As your child gets older, you can adapt your "special time" to suit their age.

Catching Your Child Being Good

One way of catching your child being good is noticing when they do things right rather than focusing on the mistakes they make. Notice when they remember to turn off the bathroom light without being told and say, "Thank you for remembering the bathroom light. Well done!" This will encourage them to do it again. Notice when they do their chores without being reminded and thank them. If they did their chores well, comment on it.

You don't always have to make a display of noticing and commenting on good behaviour. Sometimes a subtle gesture of acknowledgement is all you need. For example, you might notice your little one sharing a toy—there's no need to interrupt their play. Simply acknowledge it by giving them a loving touch on the back or shoulder or ruffle their hair as you walk by.

Planned Ignoring

If your child is used to getting lots of positive attention, you can make use of a technique called "planned ignoring" for some negative behaviours. For example, your child is throwing a tantrum. Planned ignoring means that you do not react to them at all. You don't look at them, talk to them, touch them or try to make them stop in any way. Because they are not getting a reaction, they will eventually stop the behaviour. As soon as they do, you can give them positive attention by saying, "I can see you're managed to calm yourself down. Well done." If your child is old enough, you could add, "If you feel like it, we can talk about it."

Time-Out

But didn't we agree that a time-out was a form of punishment when we discussed traditional punishment methods? Then how can it be used as a form of positive discipline?

Time-out got its bad name from stories and images of kids sitting in a corner wearing a paper cone on their head with the word "dunce" on it. A child does not learn anything positive from being socially isolated and humiliated.

Time-out, when used as a positive discipline tool, has an entirely different method and outcome.

Remember, in the first chapter, one of the techniques to keep your cool was giving yourself time-out so that you can get your feelings under control? This is what you want your child to learn. You want your child to learn to take a time-out of their own accord when they find themselves in a difficult situation or need to regain control of their emotions.

You can start using time-out from as early as nine months for anything from not listening to throwing toys or hitting another child. When the child misbehaves, take or send them to a safe place such as a playpen for younger ones, or a chair or step for older kids. You are removing them from a difficult situation and giving them the opportunity to self-calm. You don't need a lot of words when you send them to time-out. All you need to do is to point to the agreed time-out area or take them there and say, "Time-out," and name what they are doing, for instance, "hitting".

It is important that they can see you and that you can see them. There shouldn't be any distractions in the area, and while you should be able to see each other, no one must interact with the child—that means talking to, looking at, or touching them.

Time-out should not go "by the clock". Your child's behaviour isn't a boiled egg that will be ready in five minutes. As soon as you notice that the child is no longer agitated, praise them for calming themselves and allow them to carry on playing or whatever they were doing. There is no need for long speeches to explain to your child what is happening. They already know.

If the child refuses to go to the agreed spot for a time-out, there is no need to say anything. Simply pick them up and put them where you want them and keep on doing that. If they keep on resisting and it becomes a power-struggle, it is time to apply planned ignoring. Do not acknowledge their bad behaviour in any way and stop trying to take them to the time-out area. Simply ignore their behaviour. Do not speak to them, touch them, or look at them directly until they have calmed their emotions and their movements. Once you see that they have regained their composure to some degree, you can speak to them and invite them to come and take a time-out until they have a quiet mouth, quiet hands, and quiet feet.

Always make sure that your child understands that they are not being punished and that they can go back and play as soon as they have control over their emotions or behaviour again.

Once your child gets older, they will begin to understand the purpose of taking a time-out. They will understand that it is an opportunity to catch their breath and regain their composure so that they can go back into a situation with a different demeanour. When they are old enough, you no longer need to send them to a time-out location. You can simply say, "Time-out." By now they will have learnt that this means that they need to remove themselves from the situation and go somewhere private to regain their composure. Help them understand that they don't have to wait for you to call" time-out" and that it is okay for them to say that they feel they need a moment.

You might agree in your family that the person who feels the need for time-out makes the letter T with their hands and then walks away. That is a signal to the other person that you are not in control right now and are going to take a few minutes to get yourself together.

Of course, time-out doesn't mean time off. If time-out was called because a discussion was getting too heated, the discussion needs to be continued once everybody has calmed down so that the problem can be resolved. It is not a good thing to leave unresolved issues hanging in the air.

6

DEVELOPING EFFECTIVE
COMMUNICATION

I f you're going to have any kind of relationship with your child, the first step is communication; communication works both ways. Some parents may think that they're communicating with their child, but all they are doing is issuing orders and instructions. Without healthy two-way communication, you cannot develop a positive relationship with your child. When they are young, it is not always easy to understand what they are trying to communicate, but this is a crucial time in their lives, and it is important for them to know that we are at least willing to listen.

Parents who respect their children make an effort to learn how to communicate with them, and it boosts their self-esteem when children feel that they are heard and that their opinions matter.

Kids begin to communicate from the moment they are born. Their cry tells their parents that they are hungry, need to be changed, or sometimes just need some love and attention. It is essential to start teaching our children communication skills at an early age so that they are capable of expressing themselves clearly. Good communication skills also make a difference when it comes to verbalizing emotions.

Children communicate first with their parents, and then with their siblings if they have any. Once they become socially aware, they start communicating with other kids and adults that cross their path, and once they go to school, they will need to communicate with their classmates and teacher. A child learns to speak by mimicking the sounds made by his parents. The more you communicate with them, the earlier these skills will start to develop. One of the best ways to improve your child's communication proficiency is by reading to them. This improves their language skills and enlarges their vocabulary. Chatting comfortably with your child about what you're reading allows them to get used to articulating ideas and teaches them how to express themselves.

Interaction with other kids and siblings develops their social skills as well as their communication skills. They will be more comfortable in social situations and able to strike up a conversation and make a new friend quickly.

School activities call upon children's communication skills with presentations, class discussions, role play, and oral exams. Some schools also like to have an interview with a child during the application process, and a confident child who can express their thoughts clearly will already have an advantage. Such a child would also find written assignments and exams easier than a child who lacks communication skills.

Further, into their future, it is a fact that people with good communication skills have a better chance in the job market. Being able to understand and convey instructions, liaise with customers or suppliers and be able to report back clearly and concisely are just some of the skills that can give your child an advantage in a challenging job market.

THE ART OF LISTENING

You may have the ability to convey your message eloquently with people hanging on your every word, but if you don't know how to listen, then you don't know how to communicate.

Hearing and Listening

First of all, let's differentiate between hearing and listening. Hearing is passive. Unless you have blocked your ears with something or you have poor or no hearing, you will hear all the sounds that happen within the range that your ears can register. Listening is paying attention to what you are hearing. A dog may start barking in the distance. You're busy reading a book, and the sound intrudes into your little bubble. That is called hearing. As soon as you pay attention to the sound to try and find out what you just heard, you go from hearing to listening.

We listen in different ways for different reasons. When we're listening to music to relax, we listen in a different way from when we're listening to a podcast that contains information, we need for a test tomorrow.

Active Listening

One of the essential ways to strengthen the bond with your child is to actively listen to them when they talk to you. Active listening is a unique way of listening and responding. It is one of the most important skills you can have as a parent, teacher, or caregiver, and not just in those capacities; it will help you in your relationship with your partner, in the workplace, and everywhere you go.

When we are having a conversation with someone, we are often deciding how we are going to respond before they have even finished their sentence. We predict what they are going to say, judge its content, and decide on our response; all while they are speaking! It is no wonder that people so often misunderstand each other, and a normal conversation turns into a verbal battle.

Active listening is when you listen to what the other person has to say without judging the content. You focus on the feeling behind what they are saying and focus on that.

Your child tells you that they are the only one in their class that hasn't been invited to a birthday party. You know very well that other kids haven't been invited either, but now is not the time to point that out, and that isn't really what your child means. Your child is trying to say that they are feeling left out because they weren't invited to the party. You can help him put his feelings into words by saying, "I can see you're feeling upset about not being included."

An interesting contradiction is that while we should be actively listening, we should not act. Often, when our child is telling us something, we feel that we have to do something about it. We feel like calling the other child's mother and insisting that our child also be invited, but we shouldn't act on that feeling. Your first instinct is to protect your child, but you are taking away their power by deciding on their behalf and trying to band-aid all their troubles.

What your child needs is someone to actively listen and respond to the feelings behind their words and not judge them. All they want is acceptance of their statement, whatever it is. They do not need to be corrected, taught a lesson, or cross-questioned when they are confiding in you and sharing their feelings. No matter how petty or silly or untrue it may sound to you, to them it is real when they are telling it.

Parents who actively listen will find that their kids feel comfortable with approaching them to talk to them about things. These kids feel worthy of your attention, and they know that you respect their view of the world.

Active listening is not just letting your child talk. When you listen actively, you rephrase what they have said and say it back to them so that they can feel that you empathize and understand their plight. Doing this also often brings out the underlying issue. The conversation could go something like this:

> *Child:* I'm the only one that wasn't invited to Alice's party! I never want to speak to her again!
> *You:* You're upset because you feel left out.
> *Child:* Yes, she invited all the cool kids but she didn't invite me.
> *You:* You feel as if you're not one of the cool kids and

this makes you sad.
Child: She even invited Samantha! Samantha isn't even in our class.
You: You feel that she should have invited someone from her own class. Someone like you, maybe?
Child: Yes. Her mom said she could invite ten kids and I really wanted to go.

As the conversation progresses, you may find out that your child is feeling hurt because she feels that Alice doesn't value her friendship enough or she might even think she wasn't invited because she can't afford to buy Alice an expensive enough birthday present. These are all things you are finding out because you didn't respond to your child's first statement with: "Don't be silly. You know her mum said she could only invite ten kids. You can't go around hating people for things like that."

Below are some guidelines for you to follow when you are listening to your child:

- Open your ears and don't talk while they are talking.
- Try not to interrupt them or put words in their mouth.
- Encourage them to talk with prompts like, "Tell me more. Really? What else? Go on," and so on.
- Be ready to listen without judging.
- Listen for the feelings behind the words.
- Look at their body language. It will tell you a lot about

how they feel.
- Try to maintain eye contact with your child and repeat back to them in your own words what they have said.
- Don't rush in like a superhero to rescue them. Your child doesn't always want their problems to be solved—sometimes they just want to talk.

It is not just important for you to listen to your child. They also have to learn how to listen to you. This can be a challenge, especially when they are still young. Here are some tips on how you can help your child learn how to listen attentively.

- When you give your child instructions, make sure they are looking at you when you speak.
- Do not start speaking before you can see that you have their full attention.
- Keep it short and sweet—use as few words as possible and keep it simple. Even older children "zone out" when we carry on for too long about something.
- When you give them an instruction, ask them to repeat back to you in their own words what you said to them.
- Read them stories and discuss what you've read. Ask your child for their opinions about the characters and their behaviour and speculate with them about how the story is going to end.
- Sit with them and let them close their eyes and identify

the sounds they hear.

You can't expect your child to come to you out of the blue and confide in you if there is no foundation of trust. Your child needs to know that what they have told you is safe with you and that you respect their ideas and feelings. You can build that foundation by setting aside some time every day to talk and listen to each other. It doesn't matter when it happens, just *that* it happens. Talk about everyday affairs and be open to discussing feelings such as joy, anxiety, fear, jealousy, frustration, or whatever else comes up.

Sometimes your child will tell you something surprising or shocking, and it is crucial to control your reaction if that happens. A violent reaction could put them off talking about it further, so do your best to keep a straight face.

Finally, remember that you are first and foremost the role model that your child will base their behaviour on. They learn their first words from you, and they continue to learn to communicate by watching you when you interact with others and from the way you treat them. If you always talk to your child respectfully and they hear you talking to others with respect, they will do the same.

7

RAISING POSITIVE, CONFIDENT KIDS

A confident child is a happy child. Building confidence ensures your child's future success, contributes to their health, and equips them to deal with challenges, peer pressure and the general frustrations of daily living.

It is up to you as their parent to help your child establish a healthy self-image and build their self-confidence. It might seem like a daunting task, but in reality, it's neither complicated nor intimidating. It can be fun and can strengthen the relationship between you and your child.

SELF-ESTEEM AND SELF-CONFIDENCE

Self-esteem is how you feel about yourself. It is your level of self-love and how you value your worth in your own eyes and the eyes of others. If you have good self-esteem, you know that you are worthy and acceptable. You can express your opinions and assert yourself if necessary. People with good self-esteem can form positive relationships and are generally less inclined to stay in unhealthy ones. They are open to learning and are realistic in their expectations of themselves.

Self-confidence is your belief in your ability to do or achieve something. Your level of self-confidence often depends on the situation. You may be very confident about learning how to play tennis, but much less confident about learning how to play the piano. But if you have good self-esteem, you will be able to try both and not beat yourself up if you struggle and sometimes do not succeed.

Building self-esteem is part of the process of growing up. Babies who feel safe loved, and accepted have a better chance of growing into confident toddlers who are not afraid to try new things. When the parents of these toddlers pay attention to them and show that they're proud of their little one's achievements, it builds their self-esteem so that they can grow into capable young children who adapt well to change and can learn new skills.

However, self-esteem is not just influenced by a child's interactions with their parents, family, and social environment. Nature also plays a role; your child's natural strengths and weaknesses have a lot to do with how their self-esteem develops.

A child's temperament is part of their biological makeup, and this influences how they will experience things. A child with an easy-going temperament is much more likely to take things in their stride than a child with a more volatile temperament who will struggle more to cope with challenging situations.

Early life experiences such as illness, hospital stays, household moves, divorce, or death in the family, can affect children's beliefs and how they see themselves. Their interactions with their parents, caregivers, peers, and teachers also have a considerable influence on the development of a child's self-esteem.

There are many opportunities for kids to grow their self-esteem, and with their parents' help, most kids can grow into confident, positive, young adults.

How do you help your child build self-esteem and self-confidence?

Unconditional love: The way we treat children creates their impression of what we think of them. If you treat a child with respect and show that you love them even though they make mistakes or poor decisions, they will feel secure and confident to keep on trying.

Let them choose: It is empowering for a child to be allowed to choose, even if it's just between wearing the red or the yellow jacket today. It makes them feel that they are in control and will prepare them for the more difficult choices that life will present to them along the way.

Let them do things for themselves: It may take a little bit longer to get ready in the morning because your preschooler wants to get dressed by themself. Try to arrange your schedule so that there is time for this even though you feel that it will be faster and more efficient if you do it for them. This is how they learn and gain confidence in their skills and abilities. If they do well and get all their buttons done correctly and finishes on time, it gives you an excellent opportunity to notice this and compliment them.

Let them help: Especially at a certain age, kids love to help. This is your opportunity to give them age-appropriate tasks. A younger child can be allowed to put away the Tupperware while an older one might help you with bathing the dog.

Teach them responsibility: By assigning chores such as setting the dinner table, unloading the dishwasher, helping with folding the laundry, or even walking the dog, you are teaching your child responsibility, and this boosts their feeling of competency and helps develop their problem-solving skills.

Ask their opinion: Kids need to know that it's okay to ask for help or advice. You can teach them this by asking them for their advice or opinion in age-appropriate situations. A simple example would be to say to your child conversationally, "I really can't make up my mind about dinner tonight. What do you think, shepherd's pie or sausages and mashed potatoes?"

Join the game: Join your child when they play and let them lead. Showing them that they are worthy of your time increases their feeling of value and makes them feel that they are important.

Set an example: It is vital to keep on remembering that you are the role model for your child. They look to you for examples of how to behave and how to react and very often, they will build their self-image on the example you set. If you are continually breaking yourself down and making negative comments about yourself, your child will start doing the same. Learn to speak positively about yourself and what you are doing and your child will follow suit.

Praise often: Praising your child is critical when it comes to building their self-esteem, and there are many ways to do it. For praise to work and have a positive effect, it has to be sincere.

How to praise:

Don't be fake: Kids are a lot smarter than we think and they will instinctively know if you are insincere or over the top when you are praising them. Showering them with compliments and standard phrases like, "good job," doesn't go very far, and saying things that are obviously not true just confuses them. If your child has made you a birthday card, they will know you're insincere if you tell them they are the best artist in the world.

Find things to praise: When you are praising your child, you are doing it to boost their self-confidence and self-esteem. You do it to encourage them to try harder and confirm that they have done something that pleases you. The best way to praise your child is to point out true things. You can compliment your child on the birthday card by saying that you love the colours they used or that they remembered to put in the family dog.

Talk behind their back: Another way to praise your child is to do it "behind their back". A great way to boost your child's confidence is to let them "overhear" you saying good things about them to others. Remember to be sincere.

Don't compare: Focus on your child's performance. Don't compare them to other children by saying things like "Your drawing is better than Peter's." Instead, say that it is a good drawing and point out things that you like about it.

How do kids naturally build their self-esteem?

It is not just up to you as a parent to help your child build self-esteem and self-confidence. A lot of the things they do also work toward this, and it is essential for you to as a parent or caregiver to notice, help, and give positive feedback.

Your child is building self-esteem when they:

- Learn new skills, such as sports, music, art, or technical skills.
- Practice activities that they enjoy.
- Learn new things at school.
- Make new friends and grow their social circle.
- Help others and give to the needy.
- Succeed after working hard at something.
- Feel included in decisions.

- Feel accepted and understood.
- Get acknowledgement for outstanding performance such as good grades in school.
- Spend time with adults who treat them with respect.

CREATING A POSITIVE MINDSET

Life has its ups and downs, and we all have to learn how to cope with them. Learning at a young age to see the positive side of things helps us cope with disappointment and goes a long way toward a successful and rewarding life.

We know by now that our children watch our every move, copy us and learn from us. They watch how we behave, how we interact with others, and they also watch how we handle frustrations and disappointments. You can tell your child how to behave until you turn blue in the face, but what they will learn is not what you tell them—they will learn what you show them. They will mimic what they see you do. In the same way, they will also mimic your mindset. If you are always grumpy and pessimistic, don't be surprised if your child has a similar demeanour. If you are happy and positive, your child will reflect this.

Ways to Create a Positive Mindset in Your Kids and Your Home:

It's okay to show your emotions: Teach your kids to be comfortable with their emotions. The best way to do this is to be comfortable with your own. Kids need to know that it's okay to cry as well as to laugh. Allow them to express their sadness and their joy in whatever way comes naturally to them. Remember, what may seem like a little thing to you might be a big deal to your child. Ask your child questions to help them identify how they feel and affirm that it's okay to feel the way they do. Archaic beliefs such as "big boys don't cry" can stand in the way of your child's emotional well-being.

Cultivate a can-do attitude: Ben Franklin said, "You can do anything you set your mind to." If you can help your child learn that these words are true, they will be able to achieve whatever they set their minds to. Help them cultivate a can-do attitude with positive self-talk. Self-talk creates an internal dialogue that becomes a self-fulfilling prophecy if it is repeated often enough.

When they hit an obstacle, teach them to say things like, "I am strong. I can handle this challenge." If they have a problem, they can say, "I will keep trying. I know I can find a solution."

Teach them to focus on their strengths: Focus on what your child does well and encourage and motivate them. Help them identify their strengths by asking them to make a list of their positive personality traits and things that they are good at. The list could include things such as being helpful, being able to make others laugh, or they could be good at sports or the arts. They could put the list on their mirror or the fridge or somewhere else in the house where they can see it often and read it. This affirms their image of themself and helps to create a positive can-do attitude.

Teach them good manners and respect: Positive morals and values should be learnt from a young age. You can start by teaching them good manners. A child with good manners immediately makes a positive impression and research suggest that self-confidence, respect, tact, consideration for others, common sense, and flexibility are some of the traits that well-mannered individuals share.

While a child needs to learn respect for others, it is equally important that they learn that they deserve that same respect to be shown toward them. If they have learnt self-respect, they will naturally know this. Someone who respects themself will not allow another to disrespect them. You can set this example by ensuring that you always treat them with respect and standing up for them when they are being disrespected.

Talk positively: When kids come home from school, rather than merely asking, "How was your day?" try asking, "What was the best thing that happened at school today?" This automatically shifts the child's focus on the positive part of their day. Maybe your child had a particularly bad day, and they can't think of a single positive thing to tell you. Let them talk about what happened and try to help them find something positive that can come out of it.

Change "don'ts" to "do's": When we are correcting children, we very often focus on the incorrect behaviour. When we want them to learn to be truthful, we might say something like, "Don't tell lies, it's disrespectful."

When you keep repeating what they should *not* do, you put the focus on the incorrect behaviour. The child is not thinking about the right thing to do—they are focusing on what *not* to do, and because that is what is on their mind, they end up doing exactly what they were told *not* to. Kids think in pictures, so if you tell a young child not to run, they will have a mental picture of themselves running, and this increases their impulse to do precisely what you told them not to. What you should be saying is, "I want you to walk, please."

Say your child is pulling the cat's tail. Rather than yell, "Don't pull the cat's tail," say, "Let go of Kitty's tail. Be gentle." If it is necessary, show them what you mean by "be gentle." In the same way, you can replace "don't tell lies" with "be truthful" and "don't be rude" with "be polite" or "be respectful."

Create positive moods and moments: Kids are susceptible to their parents' moods and feelings. They pick up very quickly when you are stressed or upset, and it will rub off on them. While it is important for them to learn that you can't always be cheerful and relaxed, it is also important for them to see that you are doing something to make yourself feel better. This sets an example for them to follow. Some tried and trusted ideas for restoring your sanity include:

- taking a long walk,
- reading an inspiring book,
- listening to your favourite music,
- spending time in the garden,
- playing with a pet,
- taking a long bubble bath,
- chatting on the phone with a friend.

Eat right, feel good: A healthy body hosts a healthy mind, and good nutrition is just as important as a healthy, positive environment to set the scene for creating a positive mindset. Encourage your kids to eat healthy foods and make sure you're stocked up with lots of fruit and veggies as well as healthy drinks and snacks. Colourful foods are attractive, and this makes it appealing especially to younger children.

CONCLUSION

Your children are not your children.
They are the sons and daughters of life's
    longing for itself.
They come through you but not from you,
And though they are with you, yet they belong
    not to you.
You may give them your love but not your
    thoughts,
For they have their own thoughts.
You may house their bodies but not their souls,
For their souls dwell in the house of tomorrow,
Where you cannot visit, not even in your
    dreams.
You may strive to be like them,
But seek not to make them like you.

> *For life goes not backward nor tarries with yesterday.*
> *You are the bows from which your children*
> *As living arrows are sent forth.*
> *The archer sees the mark upon the path of the infinite,*
> *And He bends you with His might*
> *That His arrows may go swift and far.*
> *Let your bending in the archer's hand be for gladness;*
> *For even as He loves the arrow that flies,*
> *So He loves also the bow that is stable*
>
> **- (Gibran, n.d)**

This poem by the poet and philosopher, Kahlil Gibran, beautifully sums up everything you need to know about raising children. It teaches that our children are not our possessions. They belong to themselves. You may love them, cherish them, feed them, clothe them and house them that is your duty—but you may not tell them what to think or who to be.

They come from the future, and you come from the past. You are like a bow, and your child is the arrow that you shoot into life, into the future. It is your duty and your responsibility to make sure that your little "arrow" flies straight and true.

We started our journey towards positive discipline with *you*, the person responsible for raising your child and teaching and guiding them. What you teach your child and how you treat them during those first precious years will stay with them throughout their lives. It forms their character and it will be the foundation on which they build their careers, their relationships, and their future.

The poem likens you, the parent, to the bow, and your child to the arrow. The bow must be strong and resilient so that it can bend as much as is necessary when the string is pulled back so that the arrow will fly swift and far, but it also needs to be stable so that the arrow can fly straight and true. That is why it is so vital that you get to know yourself and to understand and evaluate where you stand right now as a parent. You can't redo your childhood, and you can't redo the years that are behind you. Still, you can make a decision right now to make the changes that you need to, to ensure that your child has the best possible chance at living an emotionally healthy, happy, balanced life.

You may have noticed that this book is not your traditional "how-to" with loads of steps, methods, tricks and tips. That is because positive discipline is not just a parenting style—it is a lifestyle; a way of thinking. Positive discipline teaches you to focus on the positive side of everything. It teaches positive morals and values and is based on mutual respect between the parent and the child.

You now know that discipline is not a means to punish someone, but rather a means to teach them. We have looked at the various types of discipline and seen that we sometimes inadvertently harm our children in our efforts to teach them the difference between right and wrong. Maybe for the first time, you have become aware that your child's mind works entirely differently from yours. Hopefully you understand why some of the things you tried didn't work. You realize that the lesson that you wanted to teach was misinterpreted entirely and that some of the things you say and do can create beliefs in your child that are entirely different from what you intended.

You realize now that your child is a delicate, unique individual that needs to form and grow into the best version of themselves that they can be and that it is your responsibility to guide them along their journey.

Wrapping It up

We tend to think that discipline is something that you do to a child. This is probably because generally speaking, "disciplining" a child means that you are punishing them for something that they did wrong.

The word, "discipline" means to teach, and there is a big difference between teaching a child and some of the "discipline" techniques that people have used over the ages. Many of these techniques involve shaming, hurting, isolating, or humiliating the child to "teach them a lesson." Sadly, the only lesson they learn is that it is okay to hurt someone that you love.

Because discipline is not just about the child, we started our journey toward learning about positive discipline with you, your child's guide and teacher. You are the person doing the disciplining. You must have the background knowledge to be able to identify what you are doing *now* to understand what needs to change. You cannot fix something if you don't know what is wrong. By studying the various parenting methods, you can identify your parenting style. Because it has been explained how the various methods of discipline influence your child's behaviour and their beliefs, you can understand why it is necessary to change some of your own beliefs about how you are going to raise your child in the future.

You have considered your parenting goals and come to understand the difference between long-term and short-term goals. We have agreed that sometimes, the old-style discipline methods are effective in achieving our short-term parenting goals, but that this is often to the detriment of our long-term parenting goals.

We went deep into the types of discipline to make sure that you understand how they work and what the pros and cons of each type are. We also looked at many of the common discipline tactics that parents use to get children to behave and how some of them can cause emotional problems later in life. We concluded that scaring children into doing our will is ineffective and harmful to the child. All we are doing is conditioning them with fear.

With a deeper understanding of precisely what you are doing and what you are dealing with, it is possible to understand the concept of positive discipline better. Positive discipline focuses on the behaviour of the child. The mantra of positive discipline is: There are no bad children; there is only bad behaviour. This is the most important thing to remember when you are raising your child with positive discipline.

Positive discipline teaches about being kind but firm. It teaches that we need to consider the child's emotions when they misbehave and acknowledge how they feel. But it also teaches consistency. Being firm means that you do not give in to the child. It means that you have acknowledged and validated how they feel, but they still have to accept that life doesn't always go the way you want it to.

Some of the other strategies used by parents who raise their kids with positive discipline include:

- Understanding that your behaviour can influence that of your child. When you can't get your child to change their behaviour, it's time to consider changing yours.
- Act more—talk less. Actions speak louder than words and merely taking away a toy when two kids are fighting is way more effective than yelling at them to stop.

- Keep it short and sweet. We deafen our kids with lengthy explanations and lots of words. Say what you need to in as few words as possible because kids don't have long attention spans.
- Follow through all the way. Do what you said you were going to.
- Turn mistakes into opportunities. Become actively involved in helping your child find solutions and teach them to manage situations appropriately.
- Teach your child to make choices.

Positive discipline isn't a "one size fits all" thing, and the ages and stages of a child's development are an essential consideration when it comes to how you guide their behaviour. Positive discipline begins at birth and continues throughout childhood into adult life. We see that very little real discipline is required in the early years. The gentle, loving guidance and truckloads of attention are all that is needed. As children get older, they are exposed to more external influences, and it becomes necessary to be more aware of their behaviour and provide more guidance.

Learning to communicate effectively with your child is very important and helps establish a bond of trust. The most important part of communicating is knowing how to listen, and it is you, the parent, that has to learn how to do that. There are different ways of listening, and we need to be able to differentiate what kind of listening is appropriate in a given situation.

Active listening is one of the most effective ways of strengthening the bond between you and your child. By responding to the content of their words without judgement, you build trust and confidence. Your child feels safe and is comfortable with discussing things with you because they know that you are taking them seriously.

A child who has a good self-image and is confident and secure is happy. One of the tasks that you have as a parent or caregiver is to do everything in your power to ensure that your child has good self-esteem and has the confidence to deal with challenges, peer pressure and the general frustrations of daily living. Kids have different temperaments, and they do not have the same physical and mental abilities. This, along with external influences, such as traumatic childhood experiences, will cause some kids to have less confidence or lower self-esteem than others, but there is a lot that you, as a parent, can do to help them build up their self-image.

Raising a child with positive discipline requires cultivating a positive mindset. Positive discipline focuses on all things positive and taking this further into daily life will help you on your journey. The most effective way to cultivate a positive mindset in your child is to cultivate a positive mindset in yourself. In the same way that you encourage your child with positive self-talk, you can encourage yourself. When you teach them that they are strong, they are brave, and they are valuable, remind yourself that you are these things too. We often forget about ourselves in our quest to do everything we can for our children.

Raising a child is a thrilling, scary, beautiful, rewarding adventure. It is also a huge responsibility, and we are often not aware of exactly how much we have to do with who a child becomes when they grow up. We make mistakes and harm our children because we are ignorant. It is up to you, as a parent or caregiver, to educate yourself and make sure that you are doing everything in your power to give your child the upbringing they deserve.

You have already proven that you care enough to want to make a difference to your child by reading this book. It is never too late to make a positive change, and if you take to heart and apply what you have learnt, you can be sure that over time, the effects of love and respect will begin to show and you will reap the rewards of your efforts.

We all want a better world, and we can change it, one person, at a time by raising our kids with a positive outlook, good values and morals. Kids who go out into the world with a strong foundation of integrity and a sense of decency are the ones who will make a difference and leave their mark on the world.

Thank you for reading my book. If you have enjoyed reading it perhaps you would like to leave a star rating and a review for me on Amazon? It really helps support writers like myself create more books. You can leave a review for me by scanning the QR code below:

Thank you so much.

Joanna Wells

REFERENCES

Admin. (2020, January 7). *5 Reason Why Discipline Is Important and Its Value In Our Life*. Impoff. https://impoff.com/importance-of-discipline-2/

Bhandarkar, S. (2013, November 18). *Positive Discipline 101: How to Discipline a Child in a Way That Actually Works*. A Fine Parent. https://afineparent.com/be-positive/positive-discipline.html

Carter, C. (2012, October 15). *How to Deal with Misbehaving Kids*. Greater Good. https://greatergood.berkeley.edu/article/item/deal_with_misbehaving_kids

Cherry, K. (2020, April 20). *Why Parenting Styles Matter When Raising Children*. Verywell Mind; Verywellmind. https://www.verywellmind.com/parenting-styles-2795072

Communicating well with children: tips. (2017, June 5). Raising Children Network. https://raisingchildren.net.au/toddlers/connecting-communicating/communicating/communicating-well-with-children

Cullins, A. (n.d.). *25 Things You Can Do Right Now To Build a Child's Confidence.* Big Life Journal. Retrieved July 25, 2020, from https://biglifejournal.com/blogs/blog/child-confidence

DeBrito, PhD, J. (2019, February 13). *Are You Responsible for Your Child's Bad Behavior?* Focus on the Family. https://www.focusonthefamily.com/parenting/are-you-responsible-for-your-childs-bad-behavior/

Familydoctor.org editorial staff. (2019, June 14). *What You Can Do to Change Your Child's Behavior - familydoctor.org.* Familydoctor.Org. https://familydoctor.org/what-you-can-do-to-change-your-childs-behavior/

Flowers, L. A. (2019, February 21). *Horrifying Ways Of Punishing Kids Throughout History.* Ranker. https://www.ranker.com/list/horrifying-ways-people-disciplined-kids-in-the-past/lisa-a-flowers

Focus 3. (n.d.). *What Does Discipline Mean?* Www.Focus3.Com. Retrieved July 25, 2020, from https://www.focus3.com/blog/what-does-discipline-mean

Kahlil Gibran on Children, www.katsandogz.com/gibran/onchildren.php.

Keyser, A. (n.d.). *9 Ideas to Improve Your Child's Listening Skills | WorksheetCloud*. Worksheetcloud.Com. Retrieved July 25, 2020, from https://www.worksheetcloud.com/blog/9-ideas-to-improve-your-childs-listening-skills/

Kind and Firm Parenting. (n.d.). Www.Positivediscipline.Com. Retrieved July 25, 2020, from https://www.positivediscipline.com/articles/kind-and-firm-parenting

LaScala, M. (2019a, March 8). *Positive Discipline May Be the Key to Getting Your Kids to Behave, Experts Say*. Good Housekeeping. https://www.goodhousekeeping.com/life/parenting/a26754534/positive-discipline/

LaScala, M. (2019b, April 1). *Five Types of Parenting Styles, Explained — And How They Affect Kids, According to Experts*. Good Housekeeping; Good Housekeeping. https://www.goodhousekeeping.com/life/parenting/a26987389/types-of-parenting-styles/

Morin, Amey. (2020, February 23). *How Emotion Coaching Can Help Your Family Focus on Feelings*. Verywell Family. https://www.verywellfamily.com/emotion-coaching-discipline-process-1095040

Morin, Amy. (2019a, July 1). *How to Discipline Children Without Yelling or Corporal Punishment*. Verywell Family. https://www.verywellfamily.com/what-is-gentle-discipline-1095046

Morin, Amy. (2019b, August 13). *5 Different Types of Child Discipline*. Verywell Family; Verywellfamily. https://www.verywellfamily.com/types-of-child-discipline-1095064

Nelsen, J., Nelsen Tamborski, M., & Ainge, B. (n.d.). *HOW IS POSITIVE DISCIPLINE DIFFERENT?* Www.Positivediscipline.Com. https://www.positivediscipline.com/articles/how-positive-discipline-different

Parents, Kids, and Discipline. (n.d.). WebMD; WebMD. Retrieved July 25, 2020, from https://www.webmd.com/parenting/guide/discipline-tactics#1

Smith, J. (2016, November 9). *A psychologist says parents should do these 18 things to raise a more confident child.* Business Insider. https://www.businessinsider.com/psychologist-explains-how-to-raise-a-more-confident-child-2016-11?IR=T

Stanborough, R. J. (2019, December 9). *Understanding the Stages of Child Development*. Healthline. https://www.healthline.com/health/childrens-health/stages-of-child-development#school-age

Tantrum, B. (n.d.). *Keeping Your Cool When Your Child Has Lost Theirs - Main NorthWest Trauma Counseling Page.* Www.Nwtraumacounseling.Org. Retrieved July 25, 2020, from http://www.nwtraumacounseling.org/family-resources/keeping-your-cool-when-your-child-has-lost-theirs

Trauma Tool Box for Primary Care. (2018, October 15). *How to Shape & Manage Your Young Child's Behavior*. HealthyChildren.Org. https://www.healthychildren.org/English/family-life/family-dynamics/communication-discipline/Pages/How-to-Shape-Manage-Young-Child-Behavior.aspx

Tugend, A. (n.d.). *9 Secrets of Confident Kids*. Parents. Retrieved July 25, 2020, from https://www.parents.com/toddlers-preschoolers/development/fear/secrets-of-confident-kids/

What's the Best Way to Discipline My Child? (2018, November 5). HealthyChildren.Org. https://www.healthychildren.org/English/family-life/family-dynamics/communication-discipline/Pages/Disciplining-Your-Child.aspx

Image Sources

https://unsplash.com/photos/bOVZ_f3fbQM

https://unsplash.com/photos/DUrU_bZV8So

https://unsplash.com/photos/Wr3HGvx_RSM

https://www.pexels.com/photo/woman-holding-her-head-2128817/

https://unsplash.com/photos/NPmR0RblyhQ

https://unsplash.com/photos/amkdlZFdMiA

REFERENCES

https://www.pexels.com/photo/parents-looking-at-their-baby-3584088/

https://unsplash.com/photos/p0hDztR46cw

https://unsplash.com/photos/dZYI4ga2eUA

https://unsplash.com/photos/D3H1opzzq68

https://unsplash.com/photos/OyCl7Y4y0Bk

https://unsplash.com/photos/-Xv7k95vOFA

https://unsplash.com/photos/yMg_SMqfoRU

https://unsplash.com/photos/4K2lIP0zc_k

https://unsplash.com/photos/BIk2ANMmNz4

https://unsplash.com/photos/dBiIcdxMWfE

www.ingramcontent.com/pod-product-compliance
Lightning Source LLC
Chambersburg PA
CBHW020107240426
43661CB00002B/64